Language and Society in
*La vida de Lazarillo de Tormes*

# Language and Society in
## *La vida de Lazarillo de Tormes*

HARRY SIEBER

*The Johns Hopkins University Press* ● *Baltimore and London*

Manufactured in the United States of America

The Johns Hopkins University Press, Baltimore, Maryland 21218
The Johns Hopkins Press Ltd., London

Library of Congress Catalog Card Number 78–8425
ISBN 0–8018–2121–5

Library of Congress Cataloging in Publication data
will be found on the last printed page of this book.

*for Claudia
and Diane*

# Prologue

> . . . adulescentes et qui nobiles estis, ad maiorum vestrorum
> imitationem excitabo, et qui ingenio ac virtute nobilitatem
> potestis consequi, ad eam rationem, in qua multi homines
> novi et honore et gloria floruerunt, cohortabor.
>
> *Cicero*, Pro Sestio

> Preguntado el filósofo Chilo si había en este mundo alguna
> cosa sobre la cual no tuviese juridición para destruir la
> fortuna, respondió: "Dos cosas hay en este mundo las cuales
> ni el tiempo las puede deshacer ni fortuna derrocar; es, a
> saber: la fama del hombre que está puesta en escritura y la
> verdad que está escondida; porque la verdad puédese algún
> tiempo suspender, mas al fin ha de parecer, y la escritura
> hace que tengamos en tanto agora los que somos a un
> hombre como le tenían los que entonces eran."
>
> *Antonio de Guevara*

The power of language to produce honor and glory, the identifying spaces of "new" men in "old" and entrenched societies, is perhaps the real subject investigated in the following study.[1] My primary intention, however, is not sociological; I do not take my analysis of the language of production beyond the nature of such a language, that is, beyond the various ways it is articulated in a literary text. Thus I propose no perfect homology between literature and society, for my interest lies *within* the text and,

---

[1]The *Lazarillo* has been interpreted persuasively as a comic parody of the *Homo Novus* tradition in R.W. Truman, "Lázaro de Tormes and the *Homo Novus* Tradition," *MLR* 64 (1969): 62–67: "The *Lazarillo* is a comic parody of these ideas as set out in the speeches of self-justification and self-glorification made by the low-born man. . ." (p. 65). See also Truman's "*Lazarillo de Tormes*, Petrarch's *De remediis fortunae*, and Erasmus's *Praise of Folly*," *BHS* 52 (1975): 33–53; Francisco Rico, *La novela picaresca y el punto de vista* (Barcelona, 1970), pp. 46–50; and Fernando Lázaro Carreter, *"Lazarillo de Tormes" en la picaresca* (Barcelona, 1972), pp. 178–83. For an early study of Petrarch and honor in Spain, see Américo Castro, "Algunas observaciones acerca del concepto del honor en los siglos XVI y XVII," *RFE* 3 (1916): 1–50, 357–86, esp. 382–84, where he cites Francisco de Madrid's 1510 translation of Petrarch's *De remediis*. Truman, in *"Lazarillo de Tormes,"* says that "what appears to be the case is that . . . it is the *De remediis fortunae* that provides the closest and most detailed series of parallels to what one finds in *Lazarillo de Tormes*" (p. 42).

more specifically, with the modes of operation that exist between the text and the language with which it is produced. This investigation is simultaneously, however, an inquiry into the wider social implications of the language of honor because the text itself functions as a sign of honor.[2] Lázaro de Tormes's claim to an honorable status as author of his own life is mediated by a Ciceronian notion of honor. Perhaps more than any classical figure, Cicero functioned in the Renaissance as a "living" model of the honor to be gained by the manipulation of words, by the domination and control of others through speech.[3] The power of language to effect action is simply its power to persuade. It is also the

[2]The "classic" studies of honor in Spain—Américo Castro, "Algunas observaciones"; Alfonso García Valdecasas, *El hidalgo y el honor* (Madrid, 1948); Peter N. Dunn, "Honour and the Christian Background in Calderón," in *Critical Essays on the Theatre of Calderón*, ed. Bruce W. Wardropper (New York, 1965), pp. 24–60; and Julio Caro Baroja, "Honor y vergüenza (examen histórico de varios conflictos populares)," in *La ciudad y el campo* (Madrid, 1966), pp. 63–130, to name only four—treat honor in its social, legal, and theological contexts without addressing the problem of its relationship to language. Bartolomé Bennassar, "Le vocabulaire de l'honneur," in *Valladolid au siècle d'or: Une ville de Castille et sa campagne au XVI$^e$ siècle* (Paris and the Hague, 1967), pp. 536–37, suggests a beginning. See also in this connection—but for France—Yves Castan, *Honnêteté et relations sociales en Languedoc (1715–1780)* (Paris, 1974).

[3]Lázaro Carreter, *Lazarillo,*" pp. 178–83, comments briefly on Cicero as a model ("Lázaro, otro Tulio"). For a thorough discussion of Cicero's place in the Renaissance, see Walter Ruegg, *Cicero und der Humanismus: Formale untersuchungen über Petrarca und Erasmus* (Zurich, 1946); and Jerrold E. Seigel, *Rhetoric and Philosophy in Renaissance Humanism: The Union of Eloquence and Wisdom, Petrarch to Valla* (Princeton, 1968). For the linguistic ideology of the period and its relationship to Cicero, see Karl Apel, *L'idea di lingua nella tradizione dell'umanesimo da Dante a Vico,* trans. Luciano Tosti (Bologna, 1975). Hanna E. Gray, while rhapsodic, is nonetheless accurate when she writes: "For Petrarch and his successors, Cicero's oration *Pro Archia* was a sacred text. They often cited or adapted the passage which celebrated the role of letters as bestowing glory upon subject and author alike, maintaining that letters provide the best, even the exclusive vehicle of immortality for men, deeds, and ideas," ("Renaissance Humanism: The Pursuit of Eloquence," in *Renaissance Essays from the Journal of the History of Ideas,* ed. Paul O. Kristeller and Philip P. Wiener [New York, 1968], p. 205). The power of speech to bring about virtually any desired goal is a topic that appears in two interesting Spanish texts of the sixteenth century. The first is Bernardo Pérez de Chinchón's 1533 translation of Erasmus's *Lingua*: "Es tanta la fuerça de la lengua que por ella antiguamente se juntaron los hombres a poblar ciudades y lugares; por ella se pusieron leyes; por ella se goviernan las repúblicas; por ella se rigen los exércitos; por ella se escriben las historias; ella sola es el engrudo, la liga, el ñudo que ata, sustenta y govierna a todo linage humano," (*La lengua de Erasmo nuevamente romançada por muy elegante estilo,* ed. Dorothy S. Severin [Madrid, 1975]). The second, more subversive in tone, is Diego de Hermosilla, *Diálogo de la vida de los pajes de palacio* (ca. 1573), ed. Donald Mackenzie (Valladolid, 1916): "Godoy. Presupuesto que Dios crió a los hombres libres y yguales, y les dio la redondez de la tierra en común y a nadie en particular al prinçipio de la creaçion, y despues del diluuio, como les dio vn lenguaje a todos, y tampoco consta por el testamento de Adan, padre del genero humano, que dexase ni mandase de la tierra más a vn hijo que a otro, no se puede pensar ni presumir sino despues que vinieron a poblar el mundo la soueruia y auariçia

ability to convince others of one's right to exist—to be "present"[4]—
which in turn implies one's honor, that "entitlement to a certain
treatment in return. The right to pride is the right to status . . . , and
status is established through the recognition of a certain social
identity."[5] Such an identity in the *Lazarillo de Tormes* is not Lázaro as
*pregonero* but Lázaro as writer, as *homo litteratus.*[6]

The *Lazarillo* is both the story of the "fortunas y adversidades"
experienced in becoming a dishonorable *pregonero* and the story of a
*pregonero* who becomes an honorable author. The totally oral status of
Lázaro as town crier of Toledo is converted into his "persona" (p. 89) as
writer.[7] The mystery that stands behind such a conversion is the same
mystery that is hidden in the language of the eucharistic formula *Hoc
est corpus meum*, in which, according to a recent analysis, "la parole

---

con sus hijas y parentela, trayendo consigo por repartidores a sus vezinos 'mio' y 'tuyo',
los que fueron anbiçiosos, *procuraron por fuerça o por buenas palabras y mañas aventajarse y
subjetar a los demas. . .*" (p. 103, emphasis mine).

[4] The phenomenological sense of the word is not read into the *Lazarillo* if we consider
his *Vida* to be an "epístola hablada" (Claudio Guillén, "La disposición temporal del
*Lazarillo de Tormes*," *HR* 25 [1957]: 268) or a "decidora epístola" (Gonzalo Sobejano, "Un
perfil de la picaresca: el pícaro hablador," in *Studia Hispanica in Honorem R. Lapesa*, 3 vols.
[Madrid, 1972], 3: 468). Antonio de Torquemada, in a relatively unknown but crucially
important text for the form of the *Lazarillo*, *Manual de escribientes* (1552), ed. María Josefa
C. de Zamora and A. Zamora Vicente (Madrid, 1970), defines the *carta* as "una mensajera
fiel de n[uest]ras yntenciones y yntérprete de los pensami[ent]os del ánimo, por la qual
hazemos ciertos a los ausentes de aquellas cosas que conuiene que nosotros les escriuamos
y que ellos entiendan y sepan *como si estando presentes se las dixiésemos por palabras, y así para
solo esto este efeto fueron ynventadas las cartas . . .*" (p. 173, emphasis mine).

[5] Julian Pitt-Rivers, "Honour and Social Status," in *Honour and Shame: The Values of
Mediterranean Society*, ed. J. G. Peristiany (Chicago, 1966), p. 22.

[6] See Apel, *L'idea di lingua*, pp. 214–19 ("La restaurazione dell'ideologia linguistica
romana"). Apel's discussion of Petrarch's reading of language as the "expressione
dell'individualità interiore" is especially pertinent for an understanding of the way in
which Lázaro's "grosero estilo" would define his individuality as writer, and hence, make
it more than a parody of the topic of *rusticitas*. Alberto Blecua, in the introduction to his
edition of *La vida de Lazarillo de Tormes y de sus fortunas y adversidades* (Madrid, 1974)—the
text that is used in this study—also says that the "grosero estilo" is more than a topical
reference: "En un prólogo normal la alusión al 'estilo grosero' no sería más que un tópico
propio del exordio. En el *Lazarillo*, el tópico cumple la función de poner al descubierto la
mentalidad del protagonista: Lázaro quiere utilizar el tópico de la *rusticitas*, cuando en
realidad no tiene otro estilo que el 'grosero', dada su condición social" (p. 43 n).
Torquemada, *Manual*, describes "el estilo torpe o grosero" as "el que no solamente tiene
en sí esta llaneza que auemos d[ic]ho, sino que tanbién ni guarda orden ni concierto ni
regla, vsando de vnos vocablos toscos y bárbaros y comunes entre gente labradora, . . . En
este género de estilo, pocas cosas se hallarán escritas, avnque ay algunos que, conforme a
lo que agora he d[ic]ho, tratan materias muy delicadas, . ."(p. 194). The "estilo grosero,"
like the "estilo ilano," is an individualizing style in that the secretary identifies himself as
author: "que cada vno se puerde nonbrar a sí mesmo por autor" (*ibid.*).

[7] The use of the word *persona* may also point to the rhetorical nature of Lázaro's *Vida*

s'égale à l'être, les mots valent pour les choses, le discours articule le monde."[8] In his communications with Vuestra Merced, the figure to whom his autobiography is addressed, Lázaro audaciously holds up his self orally defined as town crier. Autobiography is not merely verbal self-creation but also self-conversion: Lázaro turns himself into metaphor.

It is the story of this process, of these successive acts of mobilizing language, that constitutes both the subject of my essay and the hidden discourse of Lázaro's *Vida*. The nature of his "life" is not a reflection or a representation of an individualized sixteenth-century experience. Rather it is the "life" of the individualizing acts of language through which such an experience takes form. I will argue that Lázaro's "trabajos y fatigas" refer to an experience that involves a struggle with language too difficult not to be shared: " . . . muy pocos escribirían para uno solo, pues no se hace sin trabajo, y quieren, ya que lo pasan, ser recompensados, no con dineros, mas con que vean y lean sus obras" (p. 88).

The following pages attempt to retell this struggle, this process described by Emile Benveniste as the "sémantisation de la langue."[9] The mystery of the *Lazarillo*—the meaning of Lázaro's life as language—is contained in that space between Lázaro as narrating subject (writing self) and the finalized product of his narration (written

---

and to the division between, himself as Lázaro and himself as Lazarillo. Salvatore Camporeale cites and comments on the following pertinent passages from Quintilian's *Institutio oratoria*: " 'Persona, in qua de animo, corpore, extra positis quaeratur, quod pertinare ad coniecturae et qualitatis instrumenta video' (lib. III, cap. 6). La 'persona' diventa il *topos* fondamentale del discorso forense nelle 'causae judiciales': 'Initium narrationis quidam utique faciendum a persona putant' (lib. IV, c. 2), appunto perché è su di esso che si fonda l'argomentazione del retore: 'In primis igitur argumenta a persona ducenda sunt . . . ut omnia in haec duo partiamur, res atque personas' (lib. V, c. 10). Elenca poi, nel medesimo capitolo 10 del libro V—come del resto anche in altri luoghi della *Institutio*—tutti gli elementi che sono costitutivi della 'personalità,' " (*Lorenzo Valla: Umanesimo e teologia* [Florence, 1972], p. 168). Lázaro is the rhetorician of his own "caso," which is of the *admirabile genus*: "El grado de defendibilidad de una causa que choca contra el sentimiento jurídico (o generalizando por encima del campo jurídico: contra la conciencia de los valores y de la verdad) del público, se llama παραδοξον σχημα = *admirabile genus* (Quint., Isid), . ." (Heinrich Lausberg, *Manual de retórica literaria: Fundamentos de una ciencia de la literatura*, trans. José Pérez Riesco, 3 vols. [Madrid, 1966–68], 1: 113). The *caso* becomes the *persona*: Its defensibility will depend upon the extent to which Lázaro presents himself as Lazarillo. See also my analysis of the fifth *tratado*, in chapter V.

[8]Louis Marin, *La critique du discours: Sur la "Logique de Port-Royal" et les "Pensées" de Pascal* (Paris, 1975), p. 299.

[9]"L'Appareil formel de l'énonciation," *Langages* 17 (1970): 14; see also *idem*, "Sémiologie de la langue," *Semiotica* 1 (1969): 1–12, 127–35.

self). Thus at another level the novel is about itself, since one of its primary themes is the language with which it is written. Moreover, it is a self-deconstructing narrative that contains the keys to its interpretation. Our purpose is to find these interpretive keys, which function to unlock the meaning of a sequence of Lázaro's discoveries about the nature of the language that comprises his life. This means that I will not be concerned with authorship (*converso* or otherwise), sources, date of composition, influences, editorial problems, or whether or not the novel is picaresque.[10] My approach does not mean that I will ignore the conventional problems, namely, master-servant relationships, the function of folklore, thematic structure, social satire, style, and related topics. These problems, however, will be pertinent only to the extent that they provide some insight into the larger problem of language.[11]

The relationships between Lázaro and his masters, for example, will be slightly redefined in order that I may discuss their "linguistic" rather than their social implications. Lázaro learns something from each of them about the nature of language. His rite of initiation with the blind beggar is not an introduction to the world as such; it is rather his introduction to the beggar's discourse, through which an unseen world is articulated. This first *tratado* recounts the violent nature of Lázaro's semiotic initiation into the language of blindness and his appropriation and manipulation of its principal mode of enunciation (paradox), which he uses to destroy his master. The language of blindness is replaced in the second *tratado* by a sacramental discourse (a *verbum*

[10]For the relationship of the *Lazarillo* to the picaresque, see Claudio Guillén, "Luis Sánchez, Ginés de Pasamonte y los inventores del género picaresco," in *Homenaje al Prof. Rodríguez-Moñino*, 2 vols. (Madrid, 1966), 1: 221–31, reprinted with further development in his *Literature As System: Essays toward the Theory of Literary History* (Princeton, 1971), pp. 135–58; see also my *The Picaresque* (London, 1977).

[11]I wish to emphasize at this point that by "language" I mean not only a verbal (oral and written) system of signs but also sign-systems in general, which function like verbal language but with specific constraints of their own, such as money or clothes. Cf. Benveniste, "Sémiologie," p. 130: "Toute sémiologie d'un système non-linguistique doit emprunter le truchement de la langue, ne peut donc exister que par et dans la sémiologie de la langue. Que la langue soit ici instrument et non objet d'analyse ne change rien à cette situation, que commande toutes les relations sémiotiques; la langue est l'interprétant de tous les autres systèmes, linguistiques et non-linguistiques." In light of the important functions that language, money, women, and clothing play in Lázaro's *Vida*, it might have been useful to approach the novel from the viewpoint of Claude Lévi-Strauss's model of communication and exchange (see *Anthropologie structurale*, 2 vols. [Paris, 1973]). However, for the limitations of such a model and for the application of linguistics to social structures, see Georges Mounin, "Lévi-Strauss et la linguistique," in *Introduction à la sémiologie* (Paris, 1970), pp. 199–214.

*visibile*), which Lázaro fails to read properly and which leads to his victimization by the priest. Sacramental discourse is secularized in the third *tratado*: A new visible language, the *verbum visibile* of honor, determines the squire's place in a community whose sense of honor is inseparable from its economy. And in the fourth *tratado* Lázaro encounters the language of dishonor, whose communicating power is based on the implicit discourse of the symbolic. The pattern of Lázaro's linguistic life through the first four *tratados* reveals a movement that begins with his discovery of the power of speech to constitute reality and ends with his suppression of speech through his power as author, as self-censor.

The fifth *tratado* is the most important. For the first time oral and written modes of language confront one another. Speech gives way to *écriture*. The *bula*, energized by the *buldero*'s rhetoric, by his power to persuade, speaks for itself and in so doing functions as an analogue of the larger text in which it is embedded. The final *tratados* are primarily concerned with Lázaro's putting into play the operations of language that have been mastered through previous experiences. In the sixth *tratado* he combines the *verbum visibile* of honor with the economic language of Toledo's society; in the final *tratado* he returns to the language of dishonor as he attempts to silence the gossiping community around him.

The immediate purpose of his autobiography is to satisfy the request of Vuestra Merced, who has asked him to write "y relate el caso muy por extenso" (p. 89). The *caso*, narrowly defined as the scandalous sexual relationship between his wife and the archpriest,[12] is redefined at another level as the narrative relationship between Lázaro and

[12]I will argue later (in chapter VII) that Lázaro's version of the *caso* is restricted to the behavior of his wife and the archpriest; Vuestra Merced's conception of the *caso* may also include Lázaro's participation and on another level, his own as well. *Caso* has also been understood as a *caso de fortuna* (see Stephen Gilman, "The Death of *Lazarillo de Tormes*," *PLMA* 81 [1966]: 153; and Frank Durand, "The Author and Lázaro: Levels of Comic Meaning," *BHS* 45 [1968]: 93). Gilman perceives it as a "'caso de fortuna' in reverse—the rise of the lowly as against the fall of the mighty," which "introduces us to the ironical frame of commonplaces which holds the tale together." For *caso* interpreted as a *caso de honra*, see Francisco Rico, *La novela picaresca española* (Barcelona, 1967), p. 1: ". . . y'el caso' resulta ser . . . un 'caso de honra.'" (See also his recent edition of the *Lazarillo* [Barcelona, 1976], pp. 93–94.) I will introduce another definition that for reasons I will develop later may be even more pertinent: *caso* can refer to the narrative itself, especially to the epistolary narrative. See Torquemada, *Manual*, p. 215: "La narración es lo que acá comúnmente los canonistas y legistas y avn los teólogos llaman *caso*, y así, cuando quieren contar alguna cosa para venir a la determinación della, dicen: el caso es éste, y con esto van narrando o contando lo que ha sucedido o lo que sucede de presente, *ora sea verdadero, ora sea falso como si fuese verdadero*" (emphasis mine).

Vuestra Merced. Not only does Lázaro communicate (and thereby corroborate) the truth of the rumors but he simultaneously reinscribes them as part of a total life, which Vuestra Merced does *not* request. Lázaro redefines the request: The *caso* is only the point of departure for a whole and complete narration ("parescióme no tomalle por el medio, sino del principio, porque se tenga entera noticia de mi persona" [*ibid.*]). Lázaro controls the request by controlling its response. Both *caso* and *persona* are related at another level that functions to bridge his activity in the text as author and his *persona* as example. He protests the idea of a society that refuses to legitimize those individualizing acts of any person who is not born with privileged status:

> . . . y también porque consideren los que *heredaron* nobles estados cuán poco se les debe, pues Fortuna fue con ellos parcial, y cuánto más *hicieron* los que, siéndoles contraria, con fuerza y maña remando salieron a buen puerto (*ibid.*).

If we assume that Lázaro places Vuestra Merced among those who inherit and himself among those who act, we have a declaration concerning not only the modes of identity of master and servant but also their differing modes of honor. Inheritance is passivity; it is experience based on a passive mode of identity whose language is a *verbum visibile*, a visible sign system that speaks for itself, as it were, without the necessity of individualizing acts of speaking and writing. It is the language of honor embodied by the squire. It is also the language that "fails" in this novel in that those who are identified by or within its system are codified and thus anonymous.[13] The nameless Vuestra Merced and all those other characters who speak the language of institutions point to the passive nature of a nonidentifying self, a nonenunciating subject who, unlike Lázaro de Tormes, is imprisoned within preencoded linguistic systems. Their articulation of the world is in reality the already institutionalized world in which they exist.

Lázaro in the mere act of claiming the name given to him by others breaks away from encoded behavior and identity to establish his unique space within the linguistic communities of his experience.[14]

[13]Torquemada (*ibid.*, p. 200) refers to the restrictive, conventional style of *secretarios*, whose identity is hidden behind the anonymity of the institutional language of letter writing: " . . . lo que vemos es vn estilo tan hordinario en las cartas de los secretarios, como vos lo aueis d[ic]ho, que quando tratan vna materia cási todas van con vnas mesmas razones y de una mesma manera, y apenas tienen camino ni senda abierta por donde puedan subir ni vaxar ni rodear, y así forçosamente tiran su camino derecho vnas tras otras como hilera de grullas o de soldados quando van en ordenança."

[14]"Pues sepa Vuestra Mercid ante todas cosas que a mí llaman Lázaro de Tormes. . ."

The anonymity of *langue* (world) gives way to *parole* (individual) through specific acts of enunciation.[15] For Lázaro such activity (*hacer* > "hicieron") is expressed by writing. This "acting" necessarily involves appropriation both of the institutional languages of his masters and of *langue* in order to "réferer par le discours, et, chez l'autre [Vuestra Merced] la possibilité de co-référer identiquement, dans le consensus pragmatique qui fait de chaque locuteur un co-locuteur."[16] Thus Lázaro in the act of address identifies Vuestra Merced, individualizing him not as "Vuestra Merced" but as the recipient of his book. He is coreferent and as such shares his friend's (the archpriest's) dishonor through his servant's (Lázaro's) discourse.

Even Lázaro as author, however, must articulate his life with the language of *écriture*. He ends his *prólogo* and his book with a reference to his own activity and to those who do not inherit noble estates. The image of rowing one's boat to a safe harbor may well refer to the "fuerza y maña" he applies to acquire the "bien y favor" and the "oficio real" described in the seventh *tratado*.[17] But in the literary language of the Renaissance it points to the end of writing as an activity and to the completion of his life as a book.[18]

---

(Blecua, p. 91). Francisco Rico, "Problemas del 'Lazarillo,' " *BRAE* 46 (1966): 282, says: "Dice bien el pregonero 'a mí llaman,' porque, como se aprende después, sólo al final, en el muy concreto presente desde el que escribe, le 'llaman' efectivamente por su nombre completo. . . ." Américo Castro, "El 'Lazarillo de Tormes,' " *Hacia Cervantes*, 3d ed. (Madrid, 1967), describes the relationship between Lázaro and his nameless masters: "Por lo pronto, sólo Lazarillo posee un nombre propio; los demás personajes son figuras genéricas o típicas: un ciego, un clérigo, un escudero, un fraile, etc., sin ninguna característica individual, pese a la animación y plasticidad con que a casi todos los vemos" (p. 146).

[15]Benveniste, "L'Appareil," p. 14: "Avant l'énonciation, la langue n'est que la possibilité de la langue. Aprés l'énonciation, la langue est effectuée en une instance de discours, qui émane d'un locuteur. . . ."

[16]*Ibid.*, p. 14.

[17]Maurice Molho, ed., *Romans picaresques espagnols* (Paris, 1968), p. xxxix: "Le 'bon port' où aborde le gueux crieur public et cocu n'est qu'un havre de'infamie." Gilman, in "Death of *Lazarillo*," sees it in more general terms: "Lázaro's 'buen puerto,' so complacently described there [in the prologue] is the keystone of a structure based on vulnerability and protection, mortality and immortality" (p. 161).

[18]For the "classical" tradition see Ernst Robert Curtius, *European Literature and the Latin Middle Ages*, trans. Willard R. Trask (New York, 1953): "The Roman poets are wont to compare the composition of a work to a nautical voyage. . . . The poet becomes the sailor, his mind or his work the boat" (p. 129). Curtius further shows that "Cicero had already adopted these expressions in prose" (*ibid.*). A very popular late medieval text, Boccaccio's *De casibus virorum illustrum*, brings this metaphor together with the idea of writing as a source of fame and glory in a chapter entitled "Pauci flentes et libri conclusio": "Nam, divino munere, per tot regum labores, pericula, lacrimas et suprema exitia, exigua cimba estuosum mare sulcantes, eo ventum est quo ab initio proram

All prologues must come to an end, my own included. At one level Lázaro's *prólogo* is literally a *pro logos*, standing before—in the felicitous words of Claudio Guillén—the "epístola hablada" that follows. At another it constitutes a brief discourse about the book as object and about writing as an honorable and honorific activity. While I am unable to invoke Pliny ("dice Plinio que no hay libro, por malo que sea, que no tenga alguna cosa buena") or Cicero ("dice Tulio: 'La honra cría las artes'"), I can refer to those friends and colleagues who have contributed patiently and constructively to the composition of my own book. Javier Herrero has heard and read versions of my interpretations of the third and fourth *tratados*. Anthony Zahareas and Michael Hancher listened to an early draft of the first. My colleagues at Johns Hopkins attended a presentation of the second. The influence of Eduardo Saccone, Louis Marin, and John Irwin has been and continues to be paramount. Without their helpful suggestions regarding many theoretical matters related to language and autobiography the following pages would have existed only as an idea. Finally, my colleagues in Spanish—Alicia Borinsky, Paul R. Olson, and Elias L. Rivers—have heard the entire book in the most irritating manner, in bits and pieces without a controlling framework. I now thank them for their patience and judicious contributions and hope that the framework that emerges out of my argument is order enough.

---

direximus," in Pier Giorgio Ricci, ed., *Opere in versi, Corbaccio, Trattatello in laude di Dante, Prose latine, Epistole* [Milan and Naples, 1965], p. 888). The port that Boccaccio seeks is honor and fame through his book: ". . . honores, laudes, gloriam famamque perquirite, ut vos dignos adepta sublimitate monstretis; et si contingat deici, non vestro crimine factum appareat, sed protervia potius Fortune cuncta vertentis. Tu autem, parve liber, longum vive felixque, insignis militis Maghinardi meique tenax nominis atque fame" (*ibid.*, p. 890). The power of Fortune to which Boccaccio refers is precisely the power that Lázaro intends to overcome through the writing of his own book.

Language and Society in
*La vida de Lazarillo de Tormes*

I

Aures habent, et non audient; Nares habent, et non adorabunt.

*Psalms 115:6*

Toute la conduite de nostre vie depend de nos sens, entre lesquels celuy de la veue estant le plus vniuersel & le plus noble, il n'y a point de doute que les inuentions qui seruent a augmenter sa puissance, ne soyent des plus vtiles qui puissent estre.

*Descartes*

he most famous experience that Lazarillo has with his first master, the *ciego*, is his encounter with the stone bull. Lazarillo's head is smashed against the bull. His master instructs him with the following words: "Lázaro, llega el oído a este toro y oirás gran ruido dentro dél" (p. 96). It is not his ear that the blind beggar tells him to place against the bull, but his sense of hearing, that is, his inner ear.[1] He fails to grasp that the noise he will hear originates not in the bull but inside his own head.[2] Lazarillo has ears, but he does not hear. How is it possible for a mute object to make sound, to "speak"? It speaks, but in a different language. The pain of the bull's horn ("el dolor de la cornada" [p. 96]) is the result of Lazarillo's "simpleza," in this case his ignorance of the blind man's peculiar language. The bull's horns function as a visible sign of Lázaro's cuckoldry at the end of the novel and they point also to the *gran ruido,* the rumors of the *malas lenguas* of his neighbors, which threaten his comfortable life as Toledo's public voice. At another, more immediate level this incident hides the key to an understanding of the nature of the blind man's speech. The first chapter of Lázaro's *Vida,* a life that, we will continually remind ourselves, is only language, is ultimately an account of the narrator's semiotic initiation.[3] My purpose in this

[1] Erasmus, *Lingua,* follows the conventional distinction: The *orejas* are "instrumentos de los sentidos," whereas the *oídos* are "sentidos" (Pérez de Chinchón, *La lengua de Erasmo,* p. 16). In the sixteenth century, of course, there was no hard, absolute difference.

[2] Cf. A. D. Deyermond, *"Lazarillo de Tormes": A Critical Guide* (London, 1975), p. 48. Deyermond goes on to call this scene—among others—an example of "dramatic irony," which "involves the use by a character of words whose full import he [Lazarillo] does not grasp . . . " (p. 50).

[3] See Jonathan Culler, *Structuralist Poetics: Structuralism, Linguistics, and the Study of Literature* (Ithaca, 1975), pp. 103–9.

chapter is to define and to plot Lazarillo's awakening to the nature of the linguistic sign[4] and then to describe how he uses this new linguistic perception to destroy his master in the final episode of the *tratado*.

Lázaro's linguistic birth takes place in the first *tratado*, in which he recounts the story of his natural birth and his early years. We are immediately confronted with the fact that there are two births: his "literal" birth, "dentro del río Tormes" (p. 91), and his "metaphorical" birth, which occurs just before he crosses the bridge over the same river. The second birth is more important for our argument, and we will return to it later. For the moment, however, it is imperative that we interpret Lázaro's double birth in the light of the fact that he has four fathers. The first is Tomé González, who is caught stealing, exiled, and later killed in a "cierta armada contra moros" (p. 92), identified by Lazarillo's mother later in the chapter as "la de los Gelves" (p. 95). The second is his stepfather, Zaide, the "hombre moreno" (p. 93), who is the source of the "negrito muy bonito" (*ibid.*). The third is the blind beggar, who tells Lazarillo's mother that "me recibía, no por mozo, sino por hijo" (p. 95). And the fourth is God the father: " . . . después de Dios, éste [ciego] me dio la vida . . . " (p. 97). These "fathers," although different characters in the novel, nonetheless share the same function. In one way or another they are defined as paternal figures who are generating sources of Lazarillo's births. We are concerned with how and in what sense a man can be born more than once, the same mystery—but without the religious overtone—that puzzled Nicodemus: " . . . nisi quis renatus fuerit ex acqua, et Spiritu sancto, non potest introire in regnum Dei" (John 3:5). Physical birth is obviously secondary in importance, for the first *tratado* is overwhelmingly concerned with Lazarillo's painful second birth. With this perspective in mind, we can divide the chapter into three pats: (1) Lázaro's watery birth in the mill on the Tormes River; (2) his perception of his awakening to self-consciousness in witnessing his stepbrother's "mirror stage";[5] and grasp of the figurative nature of the language of blindness.

[4]Emile Benveniste, "Nature du signe linguistique," in *Problèmes du linguistique générale* (Paris, 1966), pp. 49–55: " . . . le signe, élément primordial du système linguistique, enferme un signifiant et un signifié dont la liaison doit être reconnue comme *nécessaire*, ces deux composantes étant consubstantielles l'une à l'autre. *Le caractère absolu de signe linguistique* ainsi entendu commande à son tour la *nécessité* dialectique des valeurs en constante opposition, et forme le principe structural de la langue" (p. 55).

[5]"According to J. Lacan, a phase in the constitution by the human being, occurring between the sixth and eighteenth months of life; while still in a state of impotence and motor incoordination, the child anticipates on the imaginary level the future acquisition and mastery of his bodily integrity. This imaginary integration is brought about through

[2]

Lázaro comes into the world as a link in an unbreakable chain of inherited blood. Tomé González provides his ignoble lineage and penchant for stealing. Their shared blood locks the son into a social class that has no inheritable privileges. The father's profession as a miller bespeaks thievery: If Tomé González commits "ciertas sangrías mal hechas en los costales de los que allí a moler venían" (p. 92), then Lazarillo "sangraba el avariento fardel" (p. 98) of his first master. But stealing, as Lazarillo later discovers from his stepfather's experience, is too risky to engage in extensively, for the punishment it brings is painful torture and public disgrace. Tomé González generates a situation that Lázaro never escapes. At the end of the novel Lázaro becomes his first father in the sense that he marries a woman who is as concerned with her honor as is his mother.

Antona Pérez, Lazarillo's mother, is more crucial to his life. In his father's absence she becomes the provider. She provides him not only with material goods—shelter and food—but also with a language and a domestic situation that are defined in terms of honor and profit. More importantly, she substitutes Zaide as the father in a relationship whose contractual nature implies mutual profit. Sex becomes a commodity, a currency, to be exchanged for material security and comfort:

> Yo, al principio de su entrada, pesábame con él y habíale miedo, viendo el color y mal gesto que tenía; mas de que vi que con su venida mejoraba el comer, fuile queriendo bien, porque siempre traía pan, pedazos de carne, y en el invierno leños, a que nos calentábamos (p. 93).

Antona Pérez's previous decision to "arrimarse a los buenos por ser uno dellos" (p. 92) defines Zaide as one of them and thus establishes the special context of values in which Lazarillo perceives their relationship.[6] His understanding of the network of trade-offs is not forgotten;

---

identification with the image of a similar being (*semblable*) as a total form; it is illustrated and realized by the concrete experience in which the child perceives his own image in a mirror. The mirror stage would constitute the matrix and basis of the future ego" (J. Laplanche and J.-B. Pontalis, *Vocabulaire de la psychanalyse* [Paris, 1967], translated selections by Peter Kussell and Jeffrey Mehlman in *French Freud: Structural Studies in Psychoanalysis*, Yale French Studies [New Haven, 1972], p. 192). I am aware of the so-called dangers in turning a literary text into a psychological case history. However, following the precedent of A. A. Parker's psychological reading of Quevedo's *Buscón* ("The Psychology of the *pícaro* in 'El Buscón,'" *MLR* 42 [1947]: 58–69), such an approach is justified to the extent that it produces a literary interpretation. Lacanian categories, even though taken out of context and modified in their application to the *Lazarillo*, will, I believe, provide a worthwhile interpretation of the "madre, coco" incident as well as a satisfactory explanation of Lázaro's destruction of the blind man at the end of the *tratado*.

[6]Bruce W. Wardropper, "El trastorno de la moral en el *Lazarillo*," *NRFH* 15 (1961): 442: "Los 'buenos' a quienes se allega son unos estudiantes y unos mozos de caballos del

it underlies the *caso* in which he is involved in the final chapter. His mother's last words, instructing him to be "bueno" (p. 96), reinforce the association between language and behavior that he has seen played out before his eyes.

But Lázaro's narration of the story of Zaide and his mother is not finished. Its ending involves him in a very specific way. For the first time in his short life he is made to see in a terrifying way how broadly defined this kind of contract is and its implications.[7] In the midst of domestic bliss Lazarillo is presented with a brother who functions as a representation of the constitution of self in the mirrored faces of others. Lazarillo's description of his fear upon seeing the "color y mal gesto" of his stepfather is subtly projected in the reaction of his half brother. The following scene is a retelling of Lazarillo's own "hidden" moment, in which his fear of the father is reconstituted in the linguistic relationship between his brother and his brother's father:

> Y acuérdome que estando el negro de mi padrastro trebajando con el mozuelo, como el niño vía a mi madre y a mí blancos, y a él no, huía dél con miedo para mi madre, y señalando con el dedo decía: "¡Madre, coco!" Respondió él riendo: "¡Hideputa!" (p. 93).

It is Lázaro many years later ("acuérdome") who stops the chronological unfolding of his narrative to insert this passage, thereby emphasizing it as a crucial experience in his life. He not only sees himself as Lazarillo, however; from the manner of telling and the location in the text of this anecdote we know that he also sees himself in the eyes of his brother. The complexities of the structural configuration implicit in his narration are best visualized in the following schema:

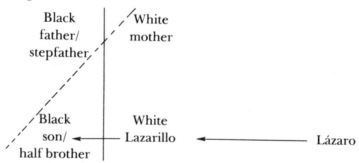

Comendador de la Magdalena . . . ." For Wardropper's more recent view of the novel, see his "The Strange Case of Lázaro Gonzáles Pérez," *MLN* 92 (1977): 202–12.

[7]Claude Lévi-Strauss would, I believe, call this kind of contract the "loi du groupe" (see *Anthropologie structurale*, 1: p. 66).

[4]

Even though he is reflecting on this incident as an adult, Lázaro emphasizes that its primary importance is to be understood in terms of his growing experience as a child: "Yo, aunque bien mochacho, noté aquella palabra de mi hermanico, y dije entre mí: '¡Cuantos debe de haber en el mundo que huyen de otros porque no se veen a sí mesmos!' " (p. 94). His brief moment of self-analysis as a "mochacho" explicitly enunciates that stage of psychic growth in which a special form of blindness ("no se veen a sí mesmos") comes into being. It is Lazarillo's brother who is blind, for within Lázaro's recasting of the memory he defines his own position as interpreter of his brother's reaction. This perceptual relation is expressed in terms of fear, in terms of the potential consequences of a threatening father. But the relationship is more complex because, as Lázaro states it, his brother's father seems to function for the brother as a mirror and not simply as a fearful father. He is not called father; he is signified rather by the word *coco*, and the important message here is one of perceived difference in the eyes of the child but sameness in the eyes of Lazarillo. The father is black; Lazarillo and his mother are white. It is even more significant that the brother flees to his white mother; this points to his blindness (he can not "see" his blackness) and to his desire to be integrated into the larger domestic community. Fear, Lázaro tells us, is the product of perceived difference and hence of the possibility of radical solitude, of being alone in the world. Zaide is dangerous in the eyes of his son precisely because he functions to separate, to sever the son from his mother and brother. The mother, then, is the mirror of the mirror stage, whereas the father is the alienating image that elicits the child's speech. Lazarillo's brother seeks to constitute himself through his language, and through the two words he speaks—"Madre, coco"—he attempts to release himself from being the same as his father by pointing to him as a frightening intruder. To summarize this process in the language of Lacanian psychoanalysis, Zaide functions as the object of "foreclosure,"[8] and Antona Pérez as the "image of a similar being" through which integration takes place ("it is illustrated and realized by the concrete experience in which the child perceives his own image in a

[8]Laplanche and Pontalis, *Vocabulaire: "Verwerfung:* the specific mechanism which would be at the origin of psychosis; it would consist of a primordial casting-out of a fundamental 'signifier' (e.g., the phallus as signifier of the castration complex) from the symbolic universe of the subject" (p. 186). "Foreclosure consists in not symbolizing that which should have been symbolized (castration): it is a 'symbolic castration' " (p. 190). The brother's attempt to cast out the father *literally* as father by reconstituting him as "coco" fails because his speech is unable to constitute reality. This is precisely the obstacle that Lázaro overcomes through his linguistic apprenticeship with the blind man.

[5]

mirror")[9] In essence Lazarillo's brother rejects his identity—that is he rejects it symbolically.[10]

The word *coco* is crucial to Lazarillo as well. His observation of the scene makes it more important than it otherwise might be. Zaide avenges the son's insult by redefining him in terms of his mother: "¡Hideputa!" (p. 93). The child's conception of the mother-father relationship is suddenly converted into a mother-son configuration: She is a whore, and Lazarillo's brother is the son of a whore. Lazarillo too is integrated into the changed relationship: He is now like his brother because they have the same whore-mother. At first Zaide is the literal father and as such merely defines the son as object; but as "coco" he becomes part of a linguistic symbolic system invented by the son, who in reconstituting him turns him into metaphor. Lazarillo is conscious of the entire process both as a child and as an adult.[11] He perceives not only the literal, genetic father-son relationship but also the subjective relationship between them and thus the language of subjectivity. If we read the mirror stage as a phase in psychic development, it represents the moment of initiation into symbolic language.

Lazarillo's brother's blindness is a result of his not perceiving the principle of sameness. For identical reasons, Lazarillo's understanding—his "insight"—of Zaide's function in terms of his own experience proceeds from the principle of difference. He recognizes that Zaide is not his real father and thus is not the same as himself. In other words, the absence (death) of his true father makes Zaide his father too. Lazarillo is as afraid of Zaide as is his brother, but he succeeds in converting him into a friendly father who provides his material comforts. Such a relationship implies not only the lack of a genetic link but the substitution of another connection with even more dangerous consequences. Lazarillo becomes Zaide's partner in crime.

[9] *Ibid.*, p. 192.

[10] The "madre, coco" scene is seen as a joke—and only as a joke—by Lázaro Carreter, *Lazarillo* (p. 109) and by Durand, "The Author and Lázaro" (p. 94), which points to the moral character of the novel. L. J. Woodward, "Author-Reader Relationship in the *Lazarillo de Tormes*," *FMLS* 1 (1965): 43–53, on the other hand, says that "Lazarillo invents this comment—indeed the whole incident is dragged in—to impress the friend of the archpriest with his sagacity even as an infant" (p. 46). I disagree with Woodward when he says that Lazarillo's observation "bears all the marks, not of childhood but of a superficial middle-aged cynicism" (*ibid.*). I simply want to make the point that jokes, especially those related to stories of parental behavior, do have a serious side. Cf. Jeffrey Mehlman, "How to Read Freud on Jokes: The Critic as *Schadchen*," *NLH* 6 (1974–75): 439–61.

[11] For an excellent analysis of the relationship between Lázaro (author) and Lazarillo (character) see Deyermond, "*Lazarillo de Tormes*," pp. 71–78.

He is ordered by his mother to sell "ciertas herraduras" (p. 94) that Zaide has stolen from the Comendador de la Magdalena. To maintain the secret domestic relationship, Lazarillo must be more than mere consumer. He must become an integral link in supplying those comforts he enjoys. Unfortunately the "conversación del Zaide" (*ibid.*) reaches the ears of the Comendador's "mayordomo, y hecha pesquisa, hallóse que la mitad por medio de la cebada que para las bestias le daban hurtaba" (*ibid.*). Zaide is caught and punished. Lazarillo's mother is brought to justice. Lazarillo, in the process of the investigation, is threatened, and because of his fear, he confesses everything he knows. Finally, as a result of the entire affair, "y por evitar peligro y quitarse de malas lenguas" (p. 95), his mother finds "legitimate" employment in a nearby "mesón."

Lazarillo has learned the cost of a comfortable, secret life, or to put it another way, he has been made aware that maintaining a materially pleasant life demands an excessive price. Lázaro's narration of this episode is not, however, an attempt to demonstrate the consequences of thievery. If it were, we would have to conclude that he had forgotten his lesson, for we find him stealing later from the beggar. The significance of Zaide's presence in the novel is found at another level. We have already seen his function in Lazarillo's perception of his brother's initiation into the symbolic nature of language. In this section Zaide functions in the much wider context of the novel as a whole. Lázaro after all is telling the story to Vuestra Merced, and in so doing he provides another entry into his autobiography from the standpoint of the final *caso*. The symmetrical relationship between the domestic arrangements in Salamanca and in Toledo is self-evident in the following diagram:

CASO

| $A$ Mayordomo | | $A_1$ Vuestra Merced | |
|---|---|---|---|
| $B$ Antona | $C$ Zaide | $C_1$ Archpriest | $B_1$ Criada |

$D$ Lazarillo $\longrightarrow$ $D_1$ Lázaro

The function of each character is determined on the basis of his identity within the organizational pattern of an identical structure. The triangle Antona-Zaide-Lazarillo is a preview of the final triangle Criada-Archpriest-Lázaro, with Lazarillo-Lázaro being the explicitly

[7]

named common denominator of both structures. In each case Lázaro perceives that it is to his material benefit to take an active role. In order to sustain a comfortable situation, he sells his stepfather's "herraduras"; he later sells the archpriest's wine and marries his "maid" because they too produce "bien y favor" (p. 174). Moreover, the secrecy of both sexual arrangements—Antona-Zaide and Criada-archpriest—becomes public knowledge in the form of gossip that comes to the attention of a person of authority: the *mayordomo* in the first instance and Vuestra Merced in the second. Investigations are forthcoming. The *mayordomo* discovers that the rumors about Zaide and Antona are true; Vuestra Merced requests Lázaro to write a report—his *Vida*—which also corroborates the truth of the *caso*. One important difference between the two incidents is that in the first the outcome is included as part of the narrative; in the second it is left unwritten. The most important difference, however, is that Zaide is clearly subservient to the *mayordomo* while Vuestra Merced is the friend and protector of the archpriest.

An understanding of Lazarillo's (and consequently Lázaro's) relationship to the story of Zaide and Antona is especially important in determining the narrative strategy that lies behind the inclusion of this story in the first place. The starting point of an analysis of relationships must begin with the fact that Lázaro includes himself in the story as Lazarillo. Lázaro's previous narration of his brother's semiotic initiation is cast in the form of an observed report in which both Lazarillo and Lázaro stand back, as it were, from the actual experience. Lazarillo observes his brother, but Lazarillo in turn is observed by Lázaro, who introduces the anecdote in order to comment on his sense of perception *as a child*. The conclusion to the story of Zaide and Antona is no longer observed by Lazarillo. He becomes part of the story and is crucial to its resolution. He stands as the focal point between Lázaro and Vuestra Merced and as such is the mediating element in their relationship as well. In what light does Lázaro place himself to be judged by Vuestra Merced? The manner in which he expresses the crime reveals an effort to create a sympathetic response on the part of his reader(s). Gathering everyone under the first-person-plural pronoun, he judges his criminal participation in comparison with the crimes of others: "No nos maravillemos de un clérigo ni fraile porque el uno hurta de los pobres y el otro de casa para sus devotas y para ayuda de otro tanto, cuando a un pobre esclavo el amor le animaba a esto" (p. 94). What Zaide did out of love for his family is no worse than the behavior of priests and friars who steal from their own *casas*. In fact, he implies, since we barely notice the friars and priests of this world who betray their professions, why should we worry about a man who, in fulfilling his responsibility to his family, is forced to steal from his employer?[12]

Lázaro's attempt to portray Zaide in a sympathetic light is simply a preview of his presentation of himself as Lazarillo: " . . . con amenazas, me preguntaban, y como niño, respondía y descubría cuanto sabía con miedo . . . " (*ibid.*). Even though he has already referred to himself as "bien mochacho," suddenly he is no more than a "niño," innocent of any wrongdoing. Unable to withhold any information out of fear, he confesses everything he knows about his mother and Zaide. Lázaro's thinly veiled dramatization in the first *tratado* of his final situation in the novel is a reference to the genesis of the *Vida* itself. Here he attempts to pull Vuestra Merced into another *ménage à trois*, one that exists at the level of narration, to define the relationship of Lázaro-archpriest-Vuestra Merced. In other words, the complicity inherent in both triangular structures functions in the same way. The contract requires that silence—the repression of *malas lenguas*—govern the relationship so that truth will not get out of hand and lead to action. The entire mechanism behind sympathy and persuasion operates on the principle of blindness / insight that Lázaro had previously elaborated. Blinding the other into believing that he is the same when in fact he is different is the basis for the kind of sympathy that Lázaro is constructing for Vuestra Merced. And this blinding is accomplished through an understanding and manipulation of a betraying mode of language that masquerades as the medium of truth.

That language—seen within the text as oral language, as speech—has the power to accomplish such a claim is indisputable when one considers Lázaro's interpretation of himself as voice.[13] The various ways in which language attains this status may not be as clear at this point as they should be; indeed, the author of the *Lazarillo* may have been aware of the subtlety of his argument, for in the final part of the first *tratado*, Lazarillo's adventures with the blind beggar, he carefully maps out in sequence the various stages that lead to Lazarillo's ability to

---

[12]Lázaro Carreter, *Lazarillo,* p. 96, asks: "¿Qué sentido puede tener tan extraño comentario, sino el de prevenir el contraste final, cuando, en la posición que antes ocupaba Zayde, hallemos un eclesiástico?" It is not so much a contrast as a comparison: Zaide steals material goods from the Comendador. I argue later that the archpriest "steals" honor from Vuestra Merced.

[13]Not only because he is writing as a *pregonero*, but also in another sense: ". . . la prosa de Lázaro en su progreso desembarazado exige adivinar, tras la letra impresa el ritmo y el tono de una voz . . ." (Rico, *La novela picaresca española,* p. lxix).

"blind" the blindman through speech. Lazarillo must perceive the principle of sameness—he must become blind like his master—before he can recognize and release himself through his appropriation of his master's language. On another level Lazarillo's apprenticeship with the beggar functions as a microcosm of the capacity of language to communicate adequately the autobiographical illusion of the self as subject.

The blind man, as I mentioned earlier, is yet another of Lazarillo's fathers. He is the most important father in this *tratado*, for the linguistic function of God as father is reserved for the second *tratado*. He is defined not so much in terms of his blindness as in terms of his speech, for it is what he teaches Lazarillo about language that pertains to the novel as a semiotic project. As a traveling speaker, he is dependent on his mouth and ears for survival.[14] His food and money are obtained through the power of his prayers and his beggar's speech:

> En su oficio era un águila: ciento y tantas oraciones sabía de coro; un tono bajo, reposado y muy sonable, que hacía resonar la iglesia donde rezaba; un rostro humilde y devoto, que con muy buen continente ponía cuando rezaba, sin hacer gestos ni visajes con boca ni ojos como otros suelen hacer (p. 97).

Moreover, Lázaro tells us, "tenía otras mil formas y maneras para sacar el dinero" (*ibid.*), all related to his artistry as a speaker. His speech acts are declarative in nature because his "words are made to fit the world at the same instant as the world is *made* to fit the words. This is because declaratives *create* the conditions to which they refer. More obviously than any other class of speech acts, they testify to the power of language to *constitute* reality." [15] Or in Lázaro's description: "Decía saber oraciones para muchos y diversos efectos: para mujeres que no parían, para las que estaban de parto, para las que eran malcasadas, que sus maridos las quisiesen bien" (*ibid.*). Lázaro of course expresses doubt about the efficacy of such prayers, but he has no doubt as to their power to produce money:" . . . ganaba más en un mes que cien ciegos en un año" (p. 98). Language in its most literal sense is seen here as a commodity to be exchanged within the defining framework of life as a

[14]To my knowledge, Charles Minguet (*Recherches sur les structures narratives dans le "Lazarillo de Tormes"* [Paris, 1970]), is the only reader who has pointed to the importance of the blind man's speech: "On . . . remarque l'importance capitale de la parole dans le succès de l'aveugle" (p. 61). Molho, *Romans picaresques espagnols*, p.xxvii, is not as impressed: ". . . ses oraisons, qu'il mesure selon l'aumône, ne sont que formules magiques dont le fidèle attend un effet immédiat."

[15]Stanley E. Fish, "How To Do Things with Austin and Searle: Speech Act Theory and Literary Criticism," *MLN* 91 (1976): 983–1025; the quotation is taken from p. 996.

marketplace.[16] "Word becomes flesh" is to be understood in an economic sense in which the corporal form of language is made visible in the alms that the blind man acquires from his unsuspecting victims. Lázaro hints that his master may have had more to offer than pious prayers, for his primary clientele comprised women: "Con esto andábase todo el mundo tras él, especialmente mujeres, que cuanto les decía, creían" (*ibid.*). While Lázaro's seemingly offhand remark about his master's sexual behavior may appear to be gratuitous, it does point to talents that exceed his linguistic artistry. Language, after all, can only establish a metaphorical union between self and others; and sexuality, as we will note later, is glossed over in near silence in the novel.

The relationship between money and speech that the blind man wants Lazarillo to perceive—speech as another kind of money—is stated at the beginning of their life together: " 'Yo oro ni plata no te lo puedo dar; mas avisos para vivir muchos te mostraré' " (p. 97). And Lazarillo adds that it is precisely his master's blindness which constitutes his point of entry into life: " . . . y siendo ciego me alumbró y adestró en la carrera de vivir" (*ibid.*). This enlightenment is brought about through a series of painful experiences, themselves a result of Lazarillo's confusion and ignorance of the inherent connection between language and blindness, between signifier and signified. The movement from *padre* to *padrastro* to his most instructive "father," the *ciego*, suggests a skeletal plot in which Lazarillo progresses from blindness to insight, from the literal nature (the real father) to the figural nature (the symbolic father) of language. If the space within which figural discourse can take place is to be produced, Lazarillo's naive perception of the singular connection between signifier and signified must be dislocated, even destroyed. The creation of this space involves a violent process that results in Lazarillo's literal destruction of his symbolic father with words.

Now in order to counter these somewhat abstract remarks, I will focus on the actualization of this process at the level of the text. Lazarillo participates in a series of tests that take the form of paradoxes.[17] He fails all of them in the sense that his inability to read them properly places him within reach of his master's victimizing

[16]See chapter III, where the concept of language / economy is more fully elaborated.

[17]Deyermond, "*Lazarillo de Tormes*," p. 46, discusses paradox as a category of style, not of structure. For a much more theoretical discussion of paradox and its relationship to the novel and to culture in general, see Eric Gans, *Essais d'esthétique paradoxale* (Paris, 1977), esp. pp. 23–59, 179–193.

hands. It is only at the end of the chapter that he succeeds in blinding his master's insight by entrapping him with his own paradox. These paradoxes can be summarized as follows: a stone bull that "speaks"; eyes that refuse to see; silence that communicates; a sausage that has no aroma. The final paradox, which Lazarillo uses to blind his master, is explicitly related to the first and last ones: a stone post that has no aroma. The *avisos* the blind beggar will teach his servant are contained in these paradoxes. At one level they are concerned with the mechanics of figurative language; at a more general level they articulate a theory of communication that characterizes the narrative strategy of Lázaro's entire autobiography.

I have briefly referred to Lazarillo's confrontation with the stone bull and to how its visible language bespeaks his role in the adulterous scene at the end of the novel. I will now describe its function in the first *tratado*. The bull literally stands at the entrance to a bridge that spans the river on which Lazarillo was born. But it stands primarily as an introduction to the series of paradoxes that follows. When Lazarillo readily obeys his master's instructions to listen to the noise that the bull will make, he does so because he believes that somehow the bull has the power to produce sound: "Yo simplemente llegué, creyendo ser ansí" (p. 96). What he believes is, not that the statue can speak, but his master's words that tell him it can speak. His sudden and painful understanding that the stone animal functions as the source of meaning of the words he has heard is an awakening to the paradoxical nature of the beggar's language. It is his sense of hearing, his ability to "hear" meaning, that is victimized. And Lazarillo's reaction to the experience indicates that it is the referential nature of the sign and not the sign itself that will determine whether or not he survives his semiotic initiation: " 'Verdad dice éste [ciego], que me cumple avivar el ojo y avisar, pues solo soy, y pensar cómo me sepa valer' " (*ibid.*). His reference to the eye is not literal; it is to the same inner eye with which blind men see. Only the metaphoric eye of blindness can read the peculiar language of blindness. Lazarillo is shown to have mastered its grammar when he deprives his blind master of his insight, emerging in the process as a consummate liar and rhetorician.

Lázaro's introduction to the polysemic nature of his master's speech is directly connected to his brother's earlier failure to perceive himself as an extension of his black father. Both experiences operate within the same conception of blindness, but with one important reversal: Lazarillo's brother is identified in the eyes of others, whereas Lazarillo—because his "father" is blind—is defined as "other" through his master's blindness. This transformation is disclosed in the next paradox, in which Lazarillo consciously blinds himself and so becomes like his "father." He must become literally blind before he can pass through his brother's stage, in which the principle of sameness implies self-recognition by becoming the other. When Lazarillo is dying for wine, he says, he fashions a long straw and uses it to secretly take his fill. His master suspects what he is doing and moves the jug between his legs. This action only encourages Lazarillo, and he manages to cut a hole in the bottom of the jug so that when his master lifts it up to drink, several drops fall into Lazarillo's waiting mouth. Not content to satisfy his thirst, he decides to turn his drinking into an esthetic experience by closing his eyes in order to enjoy it more: "Estando recibiendo aquellos dulces tragos, mi cara puesta hacia el cielo, un poco cerrados los ojos por mejor gustar el sabroso licor . . . " (p. 101). Depriving himself of his own eyesight makes him vulnerable to the beggar's insight. The jug comes crashing down on his mouth with such force that the sky—to which he had turned his face—seems to have fallen on him: " . . . me pareció que el cielo, con todo lo que en él hay, me había caído encima" (ibid.). Even though his master cures his wounds, Lazarillo now conceives of him as an alienating force to be hated: "Desde aquella hora quise mal al mal ciego" (ibid.). This emotional response is only fueled by the beggar's paradoxical conclusion to the incident: "Lo que te enfermó te sana y da salud" (p. 102).

The next paradox shifts from blindness to language itself. Lazarillo's refusal to see becomes his refusal to speak. He turns himself into a mute, believing that silence as the absence of language is also the absence of communication. Silence, however, communicates more clearly, truthfully, and loudly than speech itself, for, as Lázaro discovers at the end of his autobiography, his attempt to squelch the gossip surrounding his arrangement with the archpriest only facilitates the rumors' circulation. In this chapter his master sets up a language game, and again Lazarillo fails precisely because he is ignorant of the rules. As he and the beggar are passing a vineyard, a grape harvester (vintager) gives them a bunch of grapes.[18] In order that neither

[18]For Lázaro Carreter, Lazarillo, "la historia del racimo que viene a continuación parece traída a este lugar sólo por su belleza . . . . Sea cual sea su origen, y reconocida su escasa importancia estructural, la maestría del autor brilla, sin embargo, en el engaste" (pp. 118–19). Cf. Rico, Punto de vista, pp. 28–29: "Muy ingenioso, sin duda. Pero ¿por qué contarlo y no otra cualquiera de 'las malas burlas que el ciego burlaba'? El narrador explica así su elección: 'porque vea Vuestra Merced a cuánto se estendía el ingenio de este astuto ciego, contaré un caso de muchos que con él me acaescieron, en el cual me parece dio bien a entender su gran astucia . . . . ' Para los fines ilustrativos de Lázaro, hasta un

consumes more than the other, they agree on the following procedure: "Partillo hemos desta manera: tú picarás una vez, y yo otra; con tal que me prometas no tomar cada vez más de una uva. Yo haré lo mesmo hasta que lo acabamos, y desta suerte no habrá engaño" (p. 104). As soon as they begin eating the grapes, the beggar changes the rules by picking two at a time. Lazarillo says nothing and joins his master: "Como vi que él quebraba la postura, no me contenté ir a la par con él, mas aún pasaba adelante: dos a dos, y tres a tres" (p. 105). When the grapes are gone the beggar accuses Lazarillo of cheating. Denying his guilt, Lazarillo in the same breath admits it when he asks how his master knows. He responds: "¿Sabes en qué *veo* que las comiste tres a tres? En que comía yo dos a dos y callabas" (*ibid.*). Thinking he has taken advantage of his master's blindness, Lazarillo fails to perceive the existence of his other senses. The blind man "sees" that Lazarillo ate the grapes "tres a tres." Thus this incident is a duplication of the previous one, in which Lazarillo did not take into account the blind man's sense of touch. Here, however, the only bond of communication between them is speech. Blinded by his desire to cheat, by his pure greed, Lazarillo falls into the trap by remaining silent and thus broadcasts his thievery. If his master is to be deprived of his insight, it can not be accomplished by repressing the one talent that defines Lazarillo in later life as the voice of Toledo.

Gradually Lazarillo is learning to reduce his master's accesses to reality by cutting off his sense perceptions. The next paradox focuses on the beggar's sense of taste and smell. Lazarillo is engaged in a much larger enterprise in this episode. Up to this point he has been taken in by situations controlled, and sometimes invented, by his master. Now he takes his first steps as a creator of an extended fiction within the text, in which he attempts to control his master. Lazarillo is given a sausage that the beggar intends to cook over a fire and eat. He sends Lazarillo to a nearby tavern to buy wine, but before Lazarillo leaves on his errand, he quietly replaces the sausage with a turnip. Even though he is conscious of the sausage's aroma, his hunger is so intense that he follows through with his plan.:

> . . . no mirando qué me podría suceder, pospuesto todo el temor por cumplir con el deseo, en tanto que el ciego sacaba de la bolsa el dinero, saqué la longaniza, y, muy presto, metí el sobredicho nabo en el asador, el

---

*caso* . . . " (p. 29). Both readings are formalistic in nature and hence miss what the grape incident tells us about the nature of the blind man's *avisos*.

cual, mi amo dándome el dinero para el vino, tomó y comenzó a dar vueltas al fuego (p. 107).

Believing that if he is absent from the scene of the crime, he can not possibly be blamed as author of the fiction, he quickly eats the sausage on the way to the tavern. When his master discovers the substitution and asks Lazarillo to identify the unexpected and unseen substance, Lazarillo promptly voices his complete innocence as to its appearance, since, after all, he was not present. His mouth again is the source of his undoing; his answer is unsatisfactory. Grabbing him by the hair, his furious master jams his nose down Lazarillo's gullet. The smell of semi-digested sausage reveals Lazarillo's unsuccessful linguistic transformation: His speech is unable to transform a turnip into a sausage. Hence his carefully prepared fiction is suddenly broken apart as the blind man's probing nose locates Lazarillo's mouth, which is simultaneously the container of the sausage *and* the source of the lie. He is caught as the result of his own paradox: How can he be present to make the substitution while he is absent in the tavern?[19] In sum, the trace of his breath—the odor of his mouth—makes him present to the *ciego*. His error nearly costs him his life, but the painful outcome contains an *aviso* that provides the solution to his final linguistic encounter with his master: The language of blindness functions only at the level of metaphor. The blind man's reality must be transformed into Lazarillo's language.

As soon as Lazarillo regains his health, he and his master go begging. But because of the heavy rain, they decide to return to the inn. On the way, they encounter a swollen stream that must be crossed if they are to reach their destination. This small river reaches back to the beginning of the *tratado*, as it were, where Lazarillo and the beggar crossed a much larger river. Remembering both the experience with the stone bull and the immediately preceding sausage episode, Lazarillo's speech guides his hated master to a place from which he can leap across. Unseen by the blind man, a stone post waits on the other side. Lazarillo instructs his master to jump to safety, and believing his servant's words, the blind

[19]Woodward, in "Author-Reader Relationship," is correct, I believe, when he writes: "In the first place, all the incidents must be looked at in the light of the basic paradox: we accept that the world is subject to chance, but we simultaneously believe that we can control events by *fuerza y maña*. Secondly Lazarillo is well aware of the nature of his success, though he hopes to befuddle his readers" (p. 50). I will argue later (in chapter VII) that Lázaro is both present and absent from the scandal that has prompted Vuestra Merced's request. If we interpret *fuerza y maña* as a reference to his power as a writer we will understand better the exact nature of the success mentioned by Woodward.

man responds by smashing himself into the post. Lazarillo asks him a final question: "¿Cómo, y olistes la longaniza y no el poste?" (p. 112).

The blind beggar has a nose, but he fails to smell the post. The authority he placed in Lazarillo's words—the same authority that Lazarillo had invested in his master's words at the beginning of the *tratado*—led to the destruction of Lazarillo's symbolic father and the erection of his own linguistic system. Lazarillo's words have transformed the stone post into empty space, into language. The beggar's multiple accesses to what poses as reality in the text are steadily eliminated through language so that he is made to hear only Lazarillo's voice. Lazarillo's ability to blind through speech, to make invisible to others what is visible to himself, is acquired by learning to manipulate the language of blindness. His parting remark is evidence of the fact that stone posts do indeed have a unique odor if they are subject to linguistic transformation within a reality that is, after all, only language.

Lázaro deprives the *ciego* of his referential powers through an act of linguistic subversion. He substitutes *his* speech for the beggar's conception of the relationship between signifier and signified and thereby severs his master's understanding from an invisible world. He has broken and consequently dislocated the internal power of his master's insight.[20] In one sense he "castrates" his symbolic father as the primordial signifier by removing all linguistic mediation except his own. It is, I think, no accident that the *ciego's* sexualized nose ("metía la nariz, la cual él tenía luenga y afilada, y a aquella sazón, con el enojo, se había augmentado un palmo," [p. 108]) is countered by Lazarillo's stone column ("da con la cabeza en el poste" [P. 112]).[21] The linguistic phallus erected by Lazarillo at the end of the first *tratado* points to his mastery of figurative discourse (insight) and to the second *tratado*, in which his failure as a storyteller is a result of his own figurative blindness.

[20]This is not my metaphor: "Y en esto yo siempre le llevaba por los caminos, y adrede, por le hacer mal y daño; si había piedras, por ellas; si lodo, por lo más alto, que aunque yo no iba por lo más enjuto, holgábame a mí de quebrar un ojo por quebrar dos al que ninguno tenía" (p. 103). The only eyes that Lazarillo can break are those of his master's insight.

[21]For further sexual implications of this episode, see Javier Herrero, "The Great Icons of the *Lazarillo:* The Bull, the Wine, the Sausage and the Turnip," *Ideologies and Literature* 1, no. 5 (1978), pp. 3–18.

II

Scriptum est: Non in solo pane vivit homo, sed in omni verbo, quod procedit ore Dei.

*Matthew* 4:4

Accedit verbum ad elementum et fit Sacramentum, etiam ipsum tanquam visibile verbum.

*Saint Augustine*

azarillo's discovery and manipulation of the shifting relationships between the literal and figurative referential worlds of the *ciego's* discourse are based on his perception of the more fundamental relationship between speech and silence. His ability to blind through speech—by reconstituting reality through language— leads to self-blindness in the second *tratado*, in which his new master, an avaricious priest, possesses the insight of his former master and eyesight as well. Almost from the beginning of his life with the priest Lazarillo is aware that because the priest can see, the strategy he used against the blindman is no longer applicable:

> . . . no podía cegalle, como hacía al que Dios perdone (si de aquella calabazada feneció), que todavía, aunque astuto, con faltalle aquel preciado sentido, no me sentía, mas estotro, ninguno hay que tan aguda vista tuviese como él tenía (p. 115).

In other words, the space that defined Lazarillo's power to convert objects into language no longer exists. Merely saying that one thing is another outside the language of blindness proves to be ineffectual in removing his new master's insight. "¡Sant Juan y ciégale!" he says when the priest begins to count the remaining loaves of bread in his closely guarded chest. (p. 119) His speech is powerless to bring about the desired transformation for several reasons. The priest is not a blind man, that is, he is not literally blind and therefore is independent of Lazarillo's linguistic power. Moreover, as we will point out, Lazarillo gives up human speech by becoming mute in his metaphorical roles as mouse and serpent. Finally, if any speech act is to be effective in this *tratado*, it must form part of a continuing chain of discourse controlled by the speaker. Sustaining himself as metaphor within a fiction he generates requires that the fiction remain his own. Blinding himself to the fact that he is solely the product of his tongue places him in a

[17]

vulnerable position. At the end of the *tratado* he is viciously attacked because he fails to distinguish between those levels of language he had learned to control through his experience with the *ciego*.

Lazarillo's fictionmaking in the second *tratado* occurs in a dangerous environment. Unable to persuade the priest that one thing is another—that the steadily decreasing supply of bread is an illusion—he enters a new phase in his apprenticeship as a liar and author by creating a story over which he loses control. Casting out his net of language too far results in the formation of that small space in which his head and the priest's club will meet. His basic problem is obvious. Its solution, however, is not immediately obvious because it entails the solution of the problem posed by the entire book: How is it possible to turn oneself into language yet stand aside when that language is appropriated by others? He faces the same problem he will confront in the final *tratado* when his neighbors' gossip threatens his comfortable life—his *honra* and *provecho*—which is produced, we must remember, by his own voice as *pregonero*.

This *tratado* is not only a story of his failure as a storyteller; it is also a critical discourse, plotting the mechanism of failure to disclose the limits of figurative language. I have chosen three moments in the text that best exemplify Lazarillo's progressive blindness and self-victimization. The first is his gaining access to the priest's chest of bread; the second is his invention and experience as a mouse (the product of his own discourse); and the third is his becoming the serpent (the product of the discourse of others). The key that admits him to the chest of bread is clearly the most important element, for it also opens and closes his fiction.[1] What I will focus on specifically is how it is transformed from a literal key into Lazarillo's self-betraying tongue.[2] I will then discuss the implications of Lazarillo's self-conversion into his mouse metaphor and then into the serpent, the metaphor of the priest's neighbors. And finally I will attempt to determine what kind of language—and in what sense—constitutes the hidden center of the *tratado*.

[1] Marcel Bataillon, *Novedad y fecundidad del "Lazarillo de Tormes"* (Salamanca, 1968), states that the chest of bread is the central motif of the second *tratado*: "El episodio del clérigo avaro de Maqueda, al que no se le han hallado aún fuentes folklóricas, está fuertemente centrado por el viejo arcón de pan, por la lucha que se desarrolla en torno suyo . . . " (p. 53); José Gatti, *Introducción al "Lazarillo de Tormes"* (Buenos Aires, 1968), p. 47, and Anson Piper, "The 'Breadly Paradise' of *Lazarillo de Tormes*," *Hispania* 44 (1961): 269, agree.

[2] Bataillon, *Novedad*, p. 54: " . . . la llave escondida en la boca traicionará a su posesor, lo cual acarreará el desenlace del."

When Lazarillo enters the priest's house, he enters also a closed, interior world in which his efforts to survive are determined during the day by his master's absence and at night by his master's literal blindness. He is imprisoned by walls that can not be made invisible with words. By the end of the *tratado* those literal walls become the figurative walls of a whale's belly, in which Lazarillo is even absent from himself: "De lo que sucedió en aquellos tres días siguientes ninguna fe daré, porque los tuve en vientre de la ballena . . ." (p. 127). His hunger seems to increase as the priest's gluttony increases. After six months of starvation he is on the edge of death, so much so that, in his own words, "a abajar otro punto, no sonara Lázaro ni se oyera en el mundo" (p. 117)—he explicitly conceives of death as the absence of his voice. At this point, fortunately he believes, a *calderero* acting as *deus ex machina* appears at his master's door with a ring of keys. And while Lazarillo helps him search (with a few "flacas oraciones" [p. 118]), this angel sent by God finds the key that opens the chest.[3] The first words spoken by Lazarillo upon viewing the contents are rather extraordinary. He does not see bread as such, but "en figura de panes, como dicen, la cara de Dios" (*ibid.*). One recent translation of this passage reads, "I saw the face of God, as they say, formed by the loaves of bread." [4] Another version reads, "I saw the bread in the box, and it was like the very face of God, as they say." [5] Both translations are weak because they fail to take into account the sense of the word *figura* as prefiguration or symbol. More importantly, it is Lazarillo who emphasizes the word by using it to preface his reaction to what he sees, unwittingly suggesting a figurative interpretation, I believe, in which a connection is established "between two events or persons in such a way that the first signifies not only itself but also the second, while the second involves or fulfills the first." [6] Thus the phrase "cara de Dios" in this context may not be as innocent as the translators have made it appear. [7] Similarly we can say for the moment that the chest and key are also figurative in nature because of their association with this special bread.

[3] See Víctor García de la Concha, "La intención religiosa del *Lazarillo*," *RFE* 55 (1972): 243–77, esp. pp. 253–54.

[4] Robert S. Rudder, *The Life of Lazarillo de Tormes: His Fortunes and Misfortunes As Told by Himself with a Sequel by Juan de Luna* (New York, 1973), p. 36.

[5] Michael Alpert, *Two Spanish Picaresque Novels: "Lazarillo," "The Swindler"* (Harmondsworth, Middlesex, 1969), p. 41.

[6] Erich Auerbach, *Mimesis: The Representation of Reality in Western Literature*, trans. Willard R. Trask 1953; reprint ed., (New York, 1957), 64; see also idem, "Figura," in *Scenes from the Drama of European Literature* (New York, 1959), pp. 11–76.

[7] It is part of Lázaro's strategy to make his description of the bread look innocent by

At this point we should take a closer look at the exact nature of the bread that Lazarillo will attempt to consume, with the assumption that such an analysis will clarify not only the function of the key and chest but also the presence of the mouse and serpent later in the *tratado*. Lazarillo first describes the bread by giving it a name and identifying its source:

> El tenía un arcaz viejo y cerrado con su llave, la cual traía atada con una agujeta del paletoque, y en viniendo el bodigo de la iglesia, por su mano era luego allí lanzado, y tornada a cerrar el arca (p. 114).

The bread, then, is referred to not as "pan" but as "bodigo," that is, as the *libum votivum*. Percivale's *English-Spanish Dictionary* (1623) describes it as "a small cake or bun bread, which in diuers villages in Spaine they offer to the Priest, as also give their children." [8] It is, according to Covarrubias, "pan regalado, y en forma pequeña destos suelen llevar las mugeres por ofrenda." [9] The fact that the priest removes it from the church for his own use, together with Lazarillo's naming it "the face of God," suggests further possible interpretations. The priest has a special relationship to bread, which is defined by his role. It is through him that bread is turned into the life-giving flesh of Christ; he utters the words that trigger the mysterious process of transubtantiation. And it is precisely this role that is emphasized by Lazarillo himself near the beginning of the *tratado*: " . . . me preguntó si sabía ayudar a misa Yo dije que sí, como era verdad, que aunque maltratado, mil cosas buenas me mostró el pecador del ciego, y una dellas fue ésta" (p. 113). Soon afterward we are allowed to see the priest at work: "Cuando al ofertorio estábamos, ninguna blanca en la concha caía que no era dél registrada: el un ojo tenía en la gente y el otro en mis manos" (pp. 115–16). He is reminiscent of Lazarillo's previous master, whose

---

using the phrases "como dicen" and, later, "que ansí dicen los niños" (p. 120). Behind his playful, or parodic, attitude as author there exists an important linguistic lesson for himself as character. According to García de la Concha, we should not look beyond the parody: "Tampoco debe especularse mucho con las reiteradas anteposiciones de 'como dicen', 'ansí dicen' al sintagma 'cara de Dios'; se trata de engarzar en la parodia una costumbre popular documentada . . . " ("La intención religiosa," p. 263). It should be apparent to most readers of the *Lazarillo* that the anonymous author rarely incorporates inherited traditions without fundamental changes. Cf. Molho, "Introduction," p. xii: "Mais à partir de l'instant où Lazare de Tormes dit 'je', c'est-à-dire à l'heure même qu'il nait à la littérature, il cesse d'appartenir au folklore: rompant avec son existence antérieure de petit bonhomme facétieux, il devient le véhicule d'une pensée grave qui s'incarne en lui, qui éclate dans ses paroles et dans ses gestes moqueurs, quand bien même ils seraient ceux de la marionnette folklorique d'antan."

[8]Samuel Gili Gaya, ed., *Tesoro lexicográfico (1492–1726)*, (Madrid, 1947).
[9]Martín de Riquer, ed., *Tesoro de la lengua castellana o española*, (Barcelona, 1943).

speech also produced money. We should recall that the priest instructs Lazarillo to eat various leftovers ("los huesos roídos" [p. 115]), saying: "Toma, come, triunfa, que para ti es el mundo" (*ibid.*), a phrase whose first words suspiciously echo Christ's command to his disciples at the Last Supper: "Accipite, et comedite." Significantly perhaps, the words that complete Christ's instructions are, "Hoc est corpus meum" (Matthew 26.26).[10]

It is not necessary, however, to draw inferences from the priest's function at mass or to read excessively into the text to suggest that the bread in question is in fact holy bread. Ultimately it is beside the point, as I intend to demonstrate later. But for the sake of completeness, let us continue with Lazarillo's references. Early in the *tratado* he prays for the deaths of others "para darme vida" (p. 117); later he worships the bread, not daring, however, to receive it. . . . "comencélo de adorar, no osando rescebillo" (p. 119). He then kisses it: "Lo más que yo pude hacer fue dar en ellos mil besos . . . " (p. 120). And even later he speaks of the "persecuted" bread, and he treats the chest as if it were the body of the crucified Christ after he inflicts a gaping hole in its rib cage: " . . . luego se me rindió, y consintió, en su costado, por mi remedio, un buen agujero" (p. 122). The pierced side of the chest, which yields Lazarillo's bread of life, bespeaks an act of breaking and entering his "paraíso panal" (p. 119). Thus Lazarillo's relationship to the bread is articulated by means of a sacramental discourse. He enters paradise to contemplate the face of God.

To return to the words "cara de Dios," with which we began this digression, the late professor of medieval history Diederik Enklaar, offers an interpretation that is almost to be expected.[11] He argues that the phrase refers to the transubstantiated bread of the Sacrament and that Lazarillo's contemplation of it is an allusion to the medieval devotion of the so-called desire to view the Host as it is raised before the congregation.[12] But even here we do not have to rely on Professor

[10]Piper, "The 'Breadly Paradise,' " p. 270; García de la Concha, "La intención religiosa," suggests another biblical text—Luke 12.19: "Anima, habes multa bona posita in annos plurimos: requiesce, comede, bibe, epulare"—which is taken out of the parable of the rich miser. García de la Concha's suggestion would be a more reasonable text were it not for the fact that we are dealing with a priest—miserly or not—and with a narrative with an obviously eucharistic tone.

[11]See Juan Terlingen, "Cara de Dios," in *Studia Philologica: Homenaje ofrecido a Dámaso Alonso*, 3 vols. (Madrid, 1963), 3: 463–78. My access to Professor Enklaar's study, *Peilingen in de Beschavingsgeschiedenis van Spanje*, is through Terlingen's summary (pp. 468–69).

[12]The fundamental work on this tradition is Edouard Dumoutet's *Le désir de voir l'hostie et les origines de la dévotion au Saint Sacrament* (Paris, 1926) and his *Corpus Domini:*

Enklaar.[13] The face of God is explicitly associated with paradise in Genesis 3:8: "Et cum audissent vocem Domini Dei deambulantis in paradiso ad auram post meridiem, abscondit se Adam et uxor eius a facie Domini Dei in medio ligni paradisi." Moreover it is also related to a special bread, the *lechem panim*, which, as Luke 6:4 points out, was reserved only for the priests of the temple. Christ reminds his disciples that David ate this bread, not for religious purposes, but because he was hungry:

> Nec hoc legistis quod fecit David, cum esurisset ipse, et qui cum illo erant? Quomodo intravit in domum Dei, et panes propositionis sumpsit, et manducavit, et dedit his qui cum ipso erant: quos non licet manducare nisi tantum sacerdotibus?

Medieval and Renaissance biblical commentaries interpret the bread that David consumed in the Old Testament as a prefiguration of the bread consumed at the Last Supper in the New Testament, and David himself as a prefiguration of Christ, who releases the holy bread from the priests of the temple.[14] This is simply another way of saying that the secrecy and mystery of the inner temple will be revealed to all men in the public, visible crucifixion of Christ. And the connection between bread and paradise? That hides the mystery of our own text.

This digression is necessary to suggest that the miserly priest's bread is transformed into sacramental bread through the language that

---

*Aux sources de la piété eucharistique médiévale* (Paris, 1942).

[13]Cf. Luis de León, *De los nombres de Cristo*, ed. Federico de Onís, 3 vols. (Madrid, 1914–34), 1:83–107: " . . . conviene advertir que aunque Cristo se llama y es *cara de Dios* por donde quiera que le miremos; porque, según que es hombre, se nombre assí, y según que es Dios y en cuanto es el Verbo, es también propia y perfectamente imagen y figura del Padre . . . " (p. 93). See also Alonso de Orozco, *De nueve nombres de Cristo*, in *ibid.*, vol. III, s.v. "Del Sacramento": "Aquel pan que se ponía en una mesa de oro se llama pan de faces porque aquí en este Pan vivo se incorporan todos los escogidos" (p. 252). There is more historical interpretation of the phrase in Henry Charles Lea, *A History of Auricular Confessions and Indulgences in the Latin Church*, 3 vols. (Philadelphia, 1896), 3:502, n. 1: "This image [the Veronica] is known as the Santa Faz, or Cara de Dios, or Santo Rostro. There is another tradition, according to which Honorius III sent it to St. Ferdinand in order to encourage him in his struggle with the Infidel, but the story in the text is virtually admitted by Clement VII in a bull of December 20, 1529, granting an indulgence to the church of Jaén, confirmed by Julius III in 1553. Spain was prolific in the Santa Faz." Cf. Joseph V. Ricapito, " 'Cara de Dios': Ensayo de rectificación," *BHS* 50 (1973):142–46. Ricapito rectifies Terlingen's reading (see. 11 above: "cara de Dios" = "una buena y rica comida") by calling our attention to the "conceptos de religión, irreverencia, ironía y acaso sus puntos y ribetes de erasmismo" (p. 146).

[14]Cf. Cornelius à Lapide, *Commentaria in Lucam* Antwerp, 1681), p. 94a: " . . . sabbathum secundò primum, inquit, est sabbathum Judaeorum; hoc enim dignitate est secundum a nostro Paschate, quia post resurrectionem Christi praelatus est illi dies Dominicus: dicitur & primum, quia ante Christum erat primum & solemnissimum."

Lazarillo uses to describe it. That is, Lazarillo himself endows the bread with extraordinary meaning while attempting to consume it as ordinary bread. I am not suggesting that—despite the humorous attitudes that Lazarillo reveals toward the bread[15]—this *tratado* is a parody, or better, a travesty, of the Holy Sacrament.[16] Nor am I arguing that we should read Lazarillo's refusal and his later struggles to consume the bread as a sign of attempts by the author to ridicule the devotion of the contemplation of the Host, as Professor Enklaar believes. Rather I intend to demonstrate that the words of the institution of the Sacrament and of the second *tratado* conceal the same linguistic problem.

During the thirteenth session of the Council of Trent it was decided that a clear, straightforward definition of the doctrine of transubstantiation be formulated to counter the Protestant views, *inter alia,* of Luther and Calvin:

> 1. If any one denieth, that, in the sacrament of the most holy Eucharist, are contained truth, really, and substantially, the body and blood together with the soul and divinity of our Lord Jesus Christ, and consequently the whole Christ; but saith that He is only therein as in a sign, or in figure, or virtue; let him be anathema.
> 2. If any one saith, that, in the sacred and holy sacrament of the Eucharist, the substance of the bread and wine remains conjointly with the body and blood of our Lord Jesus Christ, and denieth that wonderful and singular conversion of the whole substance of the bread into the Body, and of the whole substance of the wine into the Blood—the species only of the bread and wine remaining—which conversion indeed the Catholic Church most aptly calls Transubstantiation; let him be anathema.[17]

---

Saint Ambrose explicitly relates David to Christ and the bread to Christ's body: " . . . quia Dauid cum sociis fugiens a facie regis Saul hic praefiguratus in lege Christus est, qui cum apostolis principem mundi lateret. Quomodo autem ille obseruator legis atque defensor panes et ipse manducauit et dedit his qui secum erant, quos non licebat manducare nisi tantummodo sacerdotibus, nisi ut per illam demonstraret figuram sacerdotalem cibum ad usum transiturum esse popularum, siue quod omnes uitam sacerdotalem debemus imitari siue quia filii ecclesiae sacerdotes sunt? Unguimur enim in sacerdotium sanctum offerentes nosmet ipsos deo hostias spirituales . . . . Quid uero euidentius quam quod in Abimelech domo quinque panes petiit Dauid, unum accepit, demonstrante typo quod iam non quinque libris, sed Christi corpore cibus fidelibus pararetur, ut Christus corpus adsumeret, ne quis de fidelibus esuriret?" (*Expositio Evangelii secundum Lucam,* ed. and trans. Dom Gabriel Tissot, O.S.B., Sources chrétiennes, vols. 45 and 52 [Paris, 1956 and 1958], 45:196—97).

[15]For example, when Lázaro touches the remaining loaves "a uso de esgremidor diestro" (p. 122).

[16]Cf.R. W. Truman, "Parody and Irony in the Self-Portrayal of Lázaro de Tormes," *MLR* 63 (1968): 600—605, where he says that Lázaro "strips religious ideas and attitudes of their solemnity for the sake of the fun of being irreverent" (p. 602).

The foundation of this entire doctrine proceeds (by way of a circuitous route through the church fathers and sixteenth-century theologians) from the words of Christ at the Last Supper. Stripping away the sacramental nature of these words, we find that Christ was engaged in making metaphor of himself in which, according to the Catholic interpretation, the signified (body) totally consumes the substances of the sign (bread). There remain only the accidents, that is, the trace of the sign. There was no room for doubt that Christ's speech, working through the priests of the Church had the power to bring about such a conversion (*conversio substantialis*). However, this pronouncement ultimately accomplished little in explaining the mechanism of transubstantiation except by faith, nor did it satisfy various Protestant theologians who sought to understand what they considered to be the real mystery hidden in the words of the institution itself. Among those who argued that Christ's words could be interpreted properly only through a linguistic analysis of the sacramental sign was Theodore Beza, a disciple of Calvin and an excellent biblical exegete in his own right.[18]

At the beginning of Beza's first significant work on the Sacraments, *Confessio Christianae Fidei* (1560), he establishes his approach. First he describes his procedure for analysis:

> There are four points which we must consider in this treatise on the sacraments: first, what sort of things signs are, and in what sense they are called signs; second, what that may be which is signified by the signs; third, the conjunction of the sign and the signified; fourth, the manner in which we grasp first the sign and then the signified *res*[19]

---

[17] J. Waterworth, trans., *The Canons and Decrees of the Sacred Oecumenical Council of Trent . . .* (London, 1848), p. 82.

[18] By my use of the word *protestant* I do not mean to imply that the anonymous author was a Protestant or that he held Protestant views of the sacraments. I am interested only in the linguistic approach of Beza's reading. For a catalogue of the representative views of the time, see Christopher Rasperger, *Duccentae verborum: "Hoc est corpus meum" interpretationes* (Ingolstadt, 1577). For an analysis of the Catholic arguments that led to the formation of the Tridentine decrees on the Eucharist, see Ferdinand Cavallera, "L'interprétation du chapitre VI de Saint Jean: Une controverse exégétique au Concile de Trente," *Revue d'Histoire Ecclésiastique* 10 (1909): 687–709, esp. pp. 694–96, where Cavallera summarizes the "interprétation spiritualiste" of the Spanish theologian Villeta; cf. Antonio Marín Ocete, *El arzobispo don Pedro Guerrero y la política conciliar española en el siglo XVI*, 2 vols. (Madrid, 1970), 1: 225–73 ("La preparación de la sesión XIII").

[19] Both text and translation are taken from Jill Raitt, *The Eucharistic Theology of Theodore Beza* (Chambersburg, Pa., 1972), p. 21: "Quatuor praecipuè consideramus in hac tractatione de Sacramentis. Primùm, quae & cuiusmodi sint signa, & quo sensu signa dicantur. Secundo, quidnam illus sit quod per illa significatur. Tertiò, quae sit signorum & rei coniunctio. Quartò, quomodo tum signa, tum res ipsas percipiamus."

By "sign" Beza does not mean the designation of something

ineffectual, as if a thing were represented to us by a picture or mere memorial figure, but to declare that the Lord . . . uses external and corporal things to represent to our external senses the greatest and most divine things, which he truly communicates to us interiorly through his Spirit: so that he does not give us the signified reality . . . less truly than he gives us the exterior and corporal signs. Again, we do not understand the word sign to refer only to the corporal element, as water in Baptism, bread and wine in the Lord's Supper: but by this name we also include those ceremonies, or rites of the mysteries, which are far from insignificant, so that we think also that nothing should be added to them or subtracted from them.[20]

Beza repeats throughout his treatise that commingling does not take place, that is, that there is, "no change of one thing into another of a totally different nature. And yet to receive the sign is to obtain the signified itself." [21] In 1576 Beza returns to the question of the Sacraments, giving a fuller development of his system of signs and its implications for the reading of sacramental discourse. Following Augustine, he redefines the sign as "that which, besides the appearance which bears upon the senses, brings something else to mind to which the sign is analogous." [22] This leads him to write that bread is not flesh, "but through the words of the institution of the sacraments a relationship is established which is clarified by the command to eat in order to have life." [23]

I will not go into Beza's further refinement and classification of signs but instead will focus on that "clarified relationship," which is

[20]*Ibid.*, p. 22: " . . . non ut inane quiddam significemus, perinde acsi res quaepiam nobis vel in pictura vel nuda quapiam nota, vel figura significaretur, set ut declaremus Dominum, pro sua insigni bonitate, externis & corporeis rebus uti, nostrae infirmitatis sublevandae causa, ad res maximas & divinissimas, quas intus nobis verè per Spiritum suum communicat, externis nostris sensibus adumbrandas: adeò ut non minus verè donet rem ipsam . . . quàm externa illa & corporea signa. Praeterea signorum vocabulo non tantùm comprehendimus corporea illa, ut aquam in Baptismo, panem et vinum in Coena Domini: sed hoc etiam nomine comprehendimus ipsas caeremonias, sive ritus ipsos mysteriorum, qui minimè sunt inanes, quò fit ut iis quoque nihil etiam addendum aut detrahendum putemus."

[21]*Ibid.*, p. 26.

[22]*Ibid.*, p. 44. Auerbach's definition of *figura* is virtually a secularization of Beza's definition of *sign*. The differences implied by Auerbach's "involves or fulfills" and Beza's "analogous" will be reconciled under Beza's definition of *metonymy*. For a more recent reading of Augustine's theory of signs, see Raffaele Simone, "Sémiologie augustinienne,"
*Semiotica* 6 (1972): 1–31; and Tzvetan Todorov, "On Linguistic Symbolism," trans. Richard Klein, *NLH* 6 (1974): 111–34.

[23]Raitt, *Eucharistic Theology*, p. 44.

implicit in this grammatical analysis of the words "hoc est corpus meum." Jill Raitt has concisely summarized Beza's analysis:

> Beza begins with a simple primary distinction: *hoc*—subject, *corpus*—attribute, *est*—copula. He then determines that *hoc* refers to what Christ was holding, namely *this bread*. The attribute is the body of Christ himself, and lest it be thought an imaginary or spiritual body, the words *which is given for you* are added. It is then the historical body born of Mary, which suffered on the cross, died, and rose, and is now seated at the right hand of the Father. This raises the question of how that body can be on earth and in heaven. The answer is that the attribute is said *figuratively* of the subject. The figure is in the copula, for the body is not figurative, nor is the bread, but the manner of attribution is figurative. This is called *metonymy*.[24]

Beza's notion of metonymy is sacramental in nature, that is, "it happens that the name of the thing signified sacramentally is attributed to the sign: or by which the sign is said to be itself that for whose signifying it is offered." [25] Beza, then, conceives of the mystery of the Sacrament as the mystery of the reading of the words of the Sacrament. We must know how to read the words of the institution in order to understand the relationship that Christ's speech is clarified: "The whole problem is solved if one will only recognize the metonymy in the words of the institution." [26] Thus when Christ says, "This bread is my body," he is saying, "This bread is sacramentally my body."

How does Beza's analysis help to direct a reading of Lazarillo's relationship, not only to the bread, but to the priest, the chest, and the key? First, the words of Lazarillo's figurative description of the bread establish a bond, a linguistic contract, between the priest and himself (and at another level, between Lázaro and Vuestra Merced): His sacramental discourse is the linguistic mediation between himself and the priest. To put it in metaphorical, more eucharistic terms, it is the structural relationship implicit in the act of Holy Communion (*koinonia*), in which the faithful are joined to the communicated body. The priest, functioning figuratively as Christ, holds the bread up before the congregation and with his words establishes the parameters of the community of language outside of which sacramental predication can not function. In other words, language redefines the participation as a function of language. We must remember, however, that it is Lazarillo and not the priest who suggests the figurative

---

[24]*Ibid.*, p. 55.
[25]*Ibid.*, p. 56: " . . . qua fit ut rei Sacramentaliter significatae nomen signo tribuatur: sive qua signum dicitur esse idipsum cui significando adhibetur. . . . "
[26]*Ibid.*, p. 60.

possibilities of the bread. It is also Lazarillo who creates the story of the mice. It is significant that he attributes the source of his fiction to God ("Dios . . . trujo a mi memoria un pequeño remedio" [p. 120]) in the same way that earlier he attributed to the Holy Spirit his lie to the tinker in order to obtain the key ("alumbrado por el espíritu Sancto" [p. 118]). God, in Lazarillo's vocabulary, stands in a metonymic relationship to Lázaro himself to express the creative and energizing power of language.[27] After thoroughly inspecting the chest, he says to himself:

> Este arquetón es viejo y grande y roto por algunas partes, aunque pequeños agujeros. Puédese pensar que ratones, entrando en él, hacen daño a este pan. Sacarlo no es cosa conveniente, porque verá la falta el que en tanta me hace vivir. Esto bien se sufre (p. 120).

Thus Lazarillo does not literally become a mouse; rather he attributes to himself the characteristics (signs) of mice. The priest knows, he says, that mice nibble bread; he will nibble it (with his fingertips) in imitation of his invention. The manner of making himself into a mouse by producing the fiction in which he will function as a mouse puts him in a special relationship to his own story. As long as the source of attribution is self-generating, as long as he is a product of himself, he retains control of the fiction as its author. It is when the manner of attribution is suggested by others, that is, when the neighbors tell the priest that a serpent is the culprit, that he loses control as author precisely because the metaphor is no longer his own. Attempting to function outside the space of sacramental predication, participating in the fiction of others, introduces the possibility of self-blinding (misreading). The neighbors, for instance, tell him how he will be trapped by telling him how the serpent has not been trapped: "Y lleva razón, que, como es larga, tiene lugar de tomar el cebo, y aunque la coja la trampilla encima, como no entre toda dentro, tórnase a salir" (p. 124). The blow will come from above. Even though he identifies himself explicitly as the serpent in question ("la culebra—o culebro, por mejor decir—no osaba roer de noche" [p. 125]), he fails to perceive the metonymy in their warning: the falling nature of the *trampilla / palo*.

The key to an understanding of the mechanism of self-blindness happens to be concealed in the key that Lazarillo acquired from the tinker. We only need to recall at this point that in order to hide it from

[27]Cf. Deyermond, *"Lazarillo de Tormes,"* p. 23: "God is equated with good luck, arranging matters so that he [Lazarillo] may gain food, money or revenge. . . . " It was indeed a strike of good luck that the tinker knocked on the door; it was God [Lazarillo] who knew what to do with him. See also García de la Concha, "La intención religiosa," pp. 247–54 ("Dios en el *Lazarillo*"); and Gilman, "Death of *Lazarillo*," p. 158.

the priest's eyesight, he places it in his mouth at night. While he is sleeping the key slips halfway out of his semilocked mouth, and breathing through it, he unconsciously emits a whistle that the priest can only interpret as the sound of the serpent. Lazarillo's literal blindness in sleep points to his figurative blindness in the fiction of the serpent. The key becomes the serpent's tongue, speaking, as it were, against the mouth in which it is found. Lazarillo's human tongue is betrayed by becoming the tongue for others, thus communicating his snake-presence to the priest.[28] His master only has to retrieve the key to compare it with his own to bring together the literal and figurative levels of the *tratado*:

> Espantado el matador de culebras qué podría ser aquella llave, miróla, sacándomela del todo de la boca, y vio lo que era, porque en las guardas nada de la suya diferenciaba. Fue luego a proballa, y con ella probó el maleficio. Debió de decir el cruel cazador: "El ratón y culebra que me daban guerra y me comían mi hacienda he hallado" (p. 127).

As an expert reader of sacramental discourse, the priest unlocks the mystery of Lazarillo's fiction. He now understands the figurative nature and thus the literal nature of the "ratón y culebra" that have consumed his bread.

Now we need to pass through one more operation to suggest what kind of language forms the hidden center of this *tratado*. Having established the nature of the key / tongue, we must look at the kind of language it speaks. The phenomenon of tongues is nowhere more thoroughly explored than in those biblical texts that stand at the margins of the second *tratado*. The confused tongues at Babel in the Old Testament and the confusing tongues at Pentecost in the New Testament contain the story of a special language. Babel is the fractionalization—in its biblically etymological sense of fragmentation (*fractio*)—of that singular prelapsarian language that allowed communication to exist among men and between men and God. Pentecost is the gathering place of these fragments in which communication takes place at another level within another sign system: The flaming tongues are visible signs that bespeak the presence of the Holy Spirit:

> Et cum complerentur dies Pentecostes, erant omnes pariter in eodem loco: et factus est repente de caelo sonus, tanquam advenientis spiritus vehementis, e replevit totam domum ubi erant sedentes. Et apparuerunt illis dispertitae linguae tanquam ignis, seditque supra singulos eorum: et

---

[28]Or to put this in other terms, Lázaro is not aware of the "creencia popular de que las culebras buscan calor en las camas de los niños" (Gatti, *Introducción*, p. 48).

repleti sunt omnes Spiritu sancto, et coeperunt loqui variis linguis, prout
Spiritus sanctus dabat eloqui illis (Acts 2.1–4).

These words (which stand as signs over all the divided tongues of
Babel) describe an interior, invisible eloquence infused by the Spirit of
God, made visible through the flaming "dispertitae linguae." This
language is privileged because its secrecy is bestowed on a chosen few.
There is, however, another language that is shared by all men in the
New Testament; the medium of deceit and betrayal, it was instrumental
in the generation of the linguistic confusion of Babel itself. It was
introduced into the world through the tongue of a serpent, and by
allowing its users to see (perceive) one another in corporeal nakedness,
it brought about their banishment from paradise. It is not a
coincidence that Lazarillo becomes a serpent in order to maintain the
bread's accessibility. Nor is it coincidental that he names the chest his
"paraíso panal." Access to it, he discovers, does not imply possession of
the bread itself. Nor does it satisfy his growing hunger; rather it
increases it:

> Mas como la hambre creciese, mayormente que tenía el estómago hecho a
> más pan aquellos dos o tres días ya dichos, moría mala muerte; tanto que
> otra cosa no hacía en viéndome solo sino abrir y cerrar el arca y contemplar
> en aquella cara de Dios . . . (p. 120).

In fact, having visible access to, but not possession of, the "cara de Dios"
leads directly to his invention of a lie that he ultimately can not sustain
and to his self-victimization at the priest's hand, the same hand that
refuses to dispense the bread of life transubstantiated through
Lazarillo's sacramental discourse. Instead this miserly hand is the force
behind the blow that silences that discourse altogether. The loss of
Lazarillo's voice is a linguistic death, a fatal misreading of the
sacramental nature of the serpent in paradise. His consumption and
contemplation of the face of God—that is, of the word of God become
flesh—precludes his understanding of it as a *visibile verbum*. He has
blinded himself to its semiotic nature by possessing it as ordinary
bread, while attributing to it extraordinary meaning. Christ said, "Ego
sum panis vitae: qui venit ad me, non esuriet, et qui credit in me, non
sitiet unquam" (John 6.35). Lazarillo confuses his literal and figurative
hungers because he fails to read properly the metonymy of his own
discourse.

The closing door at the end of the second *tratado* exiles Lazarillo
from the breadly paradise; it functions at the same time to end his
punishment in hell. The priest's final words, "No es posible sino que

[29]

hayas sido mozo de ciego" (p. 128), bind the first and second *tratados* together through blindness and language.[29] They also reveal the priest as the proper reader of sacramental discourse, because he is the repository of the mechanism of the Sacrament. For this priest there is no figurative bread, key, or serpent. His words literally produce the food that feeds his gluttony while nourishng his insight, which destroys the literal serpent. Lazarillo, then, sets himself up to be blinded by the nature of the figurative bread he creates. The shift from Lazarillo as author of his fiction to Lazarillo as its victim is an extension of the shift from metonymy to metaphor. He can not say of himself that he is both Lazarillo and the serpent in the metaphorical world that he has created for the priest. In other words, he is unable to maintain the separation between himself as author and between *culebra / culebro* and *clérigo / matador de culebras*. The priest collapses Lazarillo's linguistic project through his literal reading of its figurative discourse. Thus Lazarillo's "priestly" activities—transforming literal bread into sacramental bread—simultaneously create the space in which his master is converted from scaramental literal *clérigo* into snake hunter.

Lazarillo's conception of the relationship between God and the Holy Spirit, to whom he attributes his fiction, and the bread he attempts to consume point to another mystery concerning the nature of narrative discourse. His struggle throughout the *tratado* to possess the bread is on another level a struggle to control his verbal creation: The fragmenting bread is a sign of his disintegrating fiction. His real failure is not that he is discovered to be the mouse and the serpent but that he is identified as the motivating force behind them. Such a relationship points directly to the difficulty he encounters as author of his book: How can he be both town crier and writer, both Lázaro and Lazarillo? How can he rid himself of the dishonor of the *caso* in which he admits his participation? The solution to his problem and the mystery of his *Vida* are obvious if we perceive the metonymy of his discourse, for when he writes "This book is my life," he is saying to us as readers, "This book is sacramentally (semiotically) my life."

[29]Lázaro's attempt to cover up the despoiled bread with language echoes Augustine's interpretation of Adam and Eve's efforts to blind God with their new (linguistic) powers: " . . . ac sic ab illa illustratione veritatis ambo nudati, atque apertis oculis conscientiae ad videndum quam inhonesti atque indecori remanserint, tanquam folia dulcium fructuum, sed sine ipsis fructibus, ita sine fructu *boni operis bona verba contexunt, ut male viventes quasi bene loquendo contegant turpitudinem suam"* (*De Trinitate*, in *Patrologiae cursus completus: Series latina*, ed. J. P. Migne, 221 vols. (Paris 1844–90), vol. 42 (1886), col. 1005 [emphasis mine]).

# III

Consuetudo vero certissima loquendi magistra, utendumque plane sermone ut nummo cui publica forma est.

*Quintilian*

The non-reciprocal power semantic is associated with a relatively static society in which power is distributed by birthright and is not subject to much redistribution. The power semantic was closely tied with the feudal and manorial systems.

*R. Brown and A. Gilman*

he sacramental *verbum visibile* ("cara de Dios") that Lazarillo attempts to consume in the second *tratado* is desacramentalized, as it were, in the third, in which the bread he eats is purely secular in nature. It is obtained, not through the tongue of the serpent, but through the productive speech of begging, which he learned from the *ciego*. In the third *tratado* Lazarillo never pretends to be anyone other than himself: an obedient servant and resourceful beggar. His master, however, is the epitome of pretense. His world is in reality two worlds: the public fiction he attempts to sustain in the streets of Toledo and the private reality that exists behind the door of his rented house. His obsession with personal hygiene, clothing, residence, associates, behavior, and speech constitutes a system of signs—a language of honor—whose purpose is to insert him into the society of Toledo. He fails, or rather his language fails because he is unable to pay his rent. His words are as empty as his purse, and in a community as uncharitable and materialistic as Toledo speech and money are not interchangeable. We might say that the *escudero* embodies a "power semantic" based not on wealth but on birth. His language attempts to function in a speech community whose language is simply an extension of its economy. In this scheme Valladolid represents a static society, a "manorial system" that, through the figure of the squire, confronts the commercial system of Toledo.[1] The squire is a foreigner and speaks in

[1] The designation of these systems is based on their functions within the third *tratado*. It is interesting to note, however, that there may be some historical justification in contrasting Valladolid and Toledo in this way. See Rico, *La novela picaresca española*, p. xxxii: " . . . a mediados de siglo, en Valladolid—de donde procedía nuestro escudero—la octava parte de la población era hidalga, es decir, gozaba, por privilegio hereditario, de

a "foreign language": " . . . desde el primer día que con él asenté, le conoscí ser estranjero, por el poco conoscimiento y trato que con los naturales della [tierra] tenía" (p. 147).

Pride is the cause of the *escudero's* alien status, for it defines the most abusive and excessive aspect of the manorial system, from which he comes. He considers himself to be above everyone and thus is automatically placed outside the very system into which he seeks admission. The third *tratado* presents the struggle between these two systems—that is, between the old and the new—between the language of honor and the language of business and commerce.[2] An honorable status in Toledo, as Lazarillo will learn in this *tratado,* must be not only based on but also totally integrated within a system of production and exchange. The language of Lazarillo's beggary, for instance, functions in Toledo to produce food for both Lazarillo and his master. But it defines him as a beggar, not as an "hombre de bien." He too ends up being an outcast because of the legislation enacted to rid the city of "pobres estranjeros":

> Y fue, como el año en esta tierra fuese estéril de pan, acordaron el Ayuntamiento que todos los pobres estranjeros se fuesen de la ciudad, con pregón que el que de allí adelante topasen fuese punido con azotes. Y así ejecutando la ley, desde a cuatro días que el pregón se dio, vi llevar una procesión de pobres azotando por las Cuatro Calles. Lo cual me puso tan gran espanto, que nunca osé desmandarme demandar (pp. 143-44).

Even nature is redefined in Toledo. It is miserly and uncharitable, refusing to sustain life. The city as a closed system folds in on itself to protect its own interests. But the power of the language of civil government, in the form of a *pregón,* is overcome by the language that Lazarillo learned from his first master. He continues to feed himself in

---

ciertas libertades y exenciones tributarias"; cf. *idem,* "Problemas," pp. 293-94; and Bennassar, *Valladolid au siècle d'or,* pp. 557-67 and p. 570: "A Valladolid, pas de dynastie de marchands." Toledo housed many noble families, but in the sixteenth century it was the important economic center of Castile. See Michael Weisser, "Les marchands de Tolède dans l'économie castillane, 1565-1635," *Mélanges de la Casa de Velázquez* 7 (1971): 223-32; and *idem* "The Decline of Castile Revisited: The Case of Toledo," *The Journal of European Economic History* 2 (1973): 614-40, esp. pp. 620-21. For more detail concerning the distribution of the merchant class within Toledo, see Linda Martz and Julio Porres Martín-Cleto, *Toledo y los toledanos en 1561* (Toledo, 1974), pp. 28-29.

[2]Francisco Márquez Villanueva, "La actitud espiritual del *Lazarillo de Tormes,*" in *Espiritualidad y literatura en el siglo XVI* (Madrid, 1968), p. 96: "El gran problema del siglo XVI es que se ha entrado por las puertas un sistema económico de signo capitalista con el que no hay modo de conciliar la vieja teoría estamental." After completing this chapter, I find that Peter Dunn discusses the relationship between language and commerce in "Pleberio's World," *PMLA* 91 (1976): 406-17. Much of what he says about the *Celestina* is applicable to the *Lazarillo.*

spite of legal injunction:

> A mí diéronme la vida unas mujercillas hilanderas de algodón, que hacían
> bonetes, y vivían par de nosotros, con las cuales yo tuve vecindad y
> conocimiento. Que de la laceria que les traía me daban alguna cosilla, con la
> cual muy pasado me pasaba (p. 144).

By limiting his activities to his immediate neighbors (the same "friends"
who later come to his aid), Lazarillo creates a microsystem within the
larger, institutional system of the city that functions to bridge the gap
between the poor but "honorable" squire and the officially designated
parsimony of commerce-oriented Toledo. Lazarillo's position between
the squire and the city enables him to see the desirability of translating
his master's language of honor (Quintilian's metaphor, "sermone ut
nummo") into literal reality. In other words, Lázaro's understanding of
the contractual nature of honor and economy is based on his
observation and participation in the relationship between the squire
and Toledo. Material comforts and social status can coexist in an
economy of honor. By the final *tratado* of his *Vida* Lázaro has managed
to insert himself into such a system: His claim to honor and status is
founded on the power of his "friends," his expertise in selling the
archpriest's wine, and his decision to marry his master's concubine. His
ability to maintain such an arrangement will depend on the power of
his book to suppress the gossip that threatens his comfortable life.
Created out of his voice as town crier, Lázaro's existence is vulnerable
to the voices of others.

Lázaro, of course, later becomes the voice of Toledo, but his
introduction to the city in the third *tratado* ("di comigo en esta insigne
ciudad de Toledo" [p. 129]) is defined by all the voices of the
community: The speech he hears when he first enters the city is harsh
and direct. Barely recovered from his injury at the hands of the priest,
he is told: "—Tu, bellaco y gallofero eres. Busca, busca un amo a quien
sirvas" (p. 129). This welcome establishes the parameters of the speech
community. His low status is determined by everyone ("todos me
decían"); he is named—given identity—by a society that conceives of
him as a parasite and a rogue ("bellaco y gallofero"); and finally, he is
put in a service relationship to a superior hierarchy that demands that
he accept his position ("Busca, busca un amo"). The collective speech
addresses him with the pronoun *tú*, which emphasizes his inferiority.
The most fundamental message it communicates is clear: He can not
exist on his own outside the system; he must accept a service
relationship, offering himself in economic terms as a product to be

consumed by someone of superior standing. This hierarchical socioeconomic structure applies to everyone in Toledo but perhaps most conspicuously to the squire, who, in refusing the all-inclusive nature of this structure ends up begging from his own servant:

> Y vine a esta ciudad pensando que hallaría un buen asiento, mas no me ha sucedido como pensé. Canónigos y señores de la iglesia muchos hallo, mas es gente tan limitada, que no los sacarán de su paso todo el mundo. Caballeros de media talla también me ruegan; mas servir con éstos es gran trabajo, porque de hombre os habéis de convertir en malilla, y si no, "Andá con Dios" os dicen. Y las más veces son los pagamentos a largos plazos, y las más y las más ciertas comido por servido (pp. 150–51).

The *escudero* speaks as a servant although he wants to be served. As long as he is required to supply only *words*, he is able and willing to serve those who befit his inflated self-esteem: " . . . yo sabría mentille ['*señor de título*'] tan bien como otro, y agradalle a las mil maravillas; reille hía mucho sus donaires y costumbres, aunque no fuesen las mejores del mundo; nunca decirle cosa con que le pesase, aunque mucho le cumpliese . . . " (p. 151). But as he discovered earlier in the chapter, Toledo expects him to produce more than words. Everyone seems to demand some kind of payment, usually food or money. Lying, laughing, storytelling, flattering, and the vocabulary of love-making are not sufficient to assure oneself a space in Toledo's social system. Lazarillo sees his master "en gran recuesta con dos rebozadas mujeres, al parescer de las que en aquel lugar no hacen falta" (p. 138). The squire had turned himself into a "Macías, diciéndoles más dulzuras que Ovidio escribió" (*ibid.*). But the women of Toledo want more than verbal *dulzuras*:

> Pero, como sintieron dél que estaba bien enternecido, no se les hizo de vergüenza pedirle de almorzar con el acostumbrado pago.
> El, sintiéndose tan frío de bolsa cuanto estaba caliente del estómago, tomóle tal calofrío, que le robó la color del gesto, y comenzó a turbarse en la plática, y a poner excusas no validas (*ibid.*).

Their claim to the "acostumbrado pago" virtually deprives him of speech. His words are unable to bear up under the contractual obligation inherent in Toledo's definition of courtship.[3] And the "excusas" he attempts to substitute for the money he lacks are not acceptable as currency. He is as counterfeit as his words, and in an economy that is based on production and exchange he is quickly

---

[3]Toledo's idea of courtship at least as based on this and the final *tratado*, is synonymous with sexual promiscuity and prostitution.

discarded as a worthless investment. His poverty is an incurable sickness: "Ellas, que debían ser bien instituidas, como le sintieron la enfermedad, dejáronle para el que era" (*ibid.*).

The *escudero*'s struggle to transform speech into money as a way to enter Toledo's society remains unsuccessful throughout the chapter; as a way to escape it, however, his words succeed where previously they failed. The owners of his house and bed suddenly appear to collect their rent: "Hacen cuenta, y de dos en dos meses le alcanzaron lo que él en un año no alcanzara. Pienso que fueron doce o trece reales" (pp. 152–53). This time he pays his debt, not with the *reales* that are demanded, but with his promissory words: "Y él les dio muy buena *respuesta*: que saldría a la plaza a trocar una pieza de a dos y que a la tarde volviesen; mas su salida fue sin vuelta" (p. 153, emphasis mine). He literally gives them his *respuesta*. Merely saying that he has a "pieza de a dos" makes it so for his creditors. His words make possible his exit from Toledo. They turn out to be as negotiable ("trocar") in terms of their exchange value as the money for which they are substituted. He leaves behind the same words that he has used to manufacture the fiction of his visible public self: He is literally—and only—a man of his word.[4]

The *escudero*, then, *is* the *verbum visibile* of honor. His failure to survive in Toledo is simply a result of the fact that in Toledo's system the visible is at some point made to confront the invisible: Honorable appearance is stripped away by the dishonorable reality of poverty. It is precisely the squire's visibility, his physical presence, that attracts Lazarillo (and, obviously, the rest of the city) at the outset: " . . . topóme Dios con un escudero que iba por la calle, con razonable vestido, bien peinado, su paso y compás en orden" (p. 130). When they meet they realize simultaneously that each has need of the other: "Miróme y yo a él, y díjome: —Mochacho, ¿buscas amo? Yo le dije:—Sí, señor.—Pues vente tras mí—me respondió" (*ibid.*). It is the squire's "hábito y continente" that confirms his desirability as a master ("me parescía, según su hábito y continente, ser el que yo había menester" [*ibid.*]) and establishes his function within Lázaro's semiotic education as the representation of a primarily nonverbal system of communication. Until the master-servant relationship is reversed later in the *tratado*, the squire is as miserly with his speech as he is with his purse. It is only after

[4]The squire makes his escape by abusing "la mexor prenda" of *hidalgos* and *nobles*. Cf. Hermosilla, *Diálogo* p. 67: " . . . la mexor prenda que el hidalgo y noble han de tener en su casa, ha de ser la verdad de su palabra, por lo qual dixo vno que la promesa del hidalgo es deuda de instrumento quarentizio."

[35]

Lazarillo repeats the words of the *viuda* ("A la casa lóbrega y obscura, a la casa triste y desdichada, a la casa donde nunca comen ni beben" [pp. 146–47]) that the *escudero* reveals the full story of his life. The squire refuses to admit his poverty even in the privacy of his house; in the streets he is obsessed with the acting out of his role:

> Era de mañana cuando este mi tercero amo topé; y llevóme tras sí gran parte de la ciudad. Pasábamos por las plazas do se vendía pan y otras provisiones. Yo pensaba (y aun deseaba) que allí me quería cargar de lo que vendia, porque éste era propria hora, cuando se suele proveer de lo necesario. . . . (p. 130).

He also makes himself appear to be a devoutly religious man by not only attending mass but being the last person to leave the church:

> Desta manera anduvimos hasta que dio las once. Entonces se entró en la iglesia mayor, y yo tras él, y muy devotamente le vi oír misa y los otros oficios divinos, hasta que todo fue acabado y la gente ida. Entonces salimos de la iglesia. . . (*ibid.*).[5]

His concentration on exterior, visible signs extends to his clothes and personal hygiene: "Desque fuimos entrados, quita de sobre sí su capa, y preguntando si tenía las manos limpias, la sacudimos y doblamos, y muy limpiamente, soplando un poyo que allí estaba, la puso en él" (p. 131). The key that opened the source of life for Lazarillo in the second *tratado* now admits him to emptiness and further starvation; the house is virtually empty even though it has a "patio pequeño y razonables cámaras" (*ibid.*). Lazarillo sees only walls. Its outward appearance, like that of the squire, contrasts starkly with the interior bareness, which is emphasized by the lack of any "silleta, ni tajo, ni banco, ni mesa, ni aun tal arcaz como el de marras" (*ibid.*).

The squire's morning ritual in preparation for his public performance is comparable to the sacred dressing of a priest before administering mass.[6] First he inventories and cleans his garments: " . . . comienza a limpiar y sacudir sus calzas, y jubón, y sayo y capa. . . . Y vístese muy a su placer" (p. 136). Next comes the ceremonial washing of hands, combing of hair, and strapping on of the sword, the sign of his worth and dignity: "Echéle aguamanos, peinóse, y puso su espada

---

[5]Another strategy employed by Godoy, "criado del señor Duque," in Hermosilla's *Diálogo*, p. 115: "Quando le vuiera acauado la misa, me estuviera vn rato donde me vieran y pudieran hablar, para que el tuviera que negociar conmigo, no vuiera menester entrar por pages ni porteros. . . . "

[6]Cf. Molho, *Romans picaresques espagnols*, p. xxv: "L'écuyer professe la religion de l'honneur, qui lui est prescrite par son *hidalguía*. Honneur qui, faute de richesse, ne repose que sur l'opinion d'autrui, sur un qu'en dira-t-on qui risque de le jeter bas. . . . "

en el talabarte . . . " (*ibid.*). Fastening "un sartal de cuentas gruesas del talabarte" (*ibid.*), his last "devotional" act, he moves out into the public light "con un paso sosegado y el cuerpo derecho, haciendo con él y con la cabeza muy gentiles meneos, echando el cabo de la capa sobre el hombro y a veces so el brazo, y poniendo la mano derecha en el costado . . . "(*ibid.*). Everything—even his gestures—must be placed in the proper position and coordinated with the total image of honor. His body is simply another object to wear, to be put on as part of his costume for the drama he is about to play. It too forms part of the nonverbal system of signs—the language of honor—that is "heard" by the eyes of others.[7] And while it may sustain the fiction acted out by the squire, it is able to feed neither servant nor master. Unproductive both in obtaining an honorable position in Toledo and in securing the basic necessities for sustaining physical life, the *escudero*'s linguistic power, unlike that of a priest, is insufficient to transubstantiate the ritualistic language of honor into consumer goods. The bread he eats belongs to Lazarillo; the "wine" he offers is only water:

> . . . sacó un jarro desbocado y no muy nuevo, y desque hubo bebido, convidóme con él. Yo, por hacer del continente, dije:
> —Señor, no bebo vino.
> —Agua es—me respondió—; bien puedes beber (p. 134).

To point out the lack of an economic foundation as the cause of his master's linguistic weakness, Lázaro introduces the scene (witnessed by him) in which his master attempts to become another Macías with two of Toledo's "rebozadas mujeres" (p. 138). As mentioned above, he is unable to transform verbal *dulzuras* into edible ones because of his poverty. And in order to contrast Lazarillo's verbal power to the squire's inefficient speech, this romantic scene is followed immediately by Lazarillo's own efforts and success in converting the language he learned from the *ciego* into the food that both he and his master will eat. He has become the master:

> Desque vi ser las dos y no venía y la hambre me aquejaba, cierro mi puerta y pongo la llave do mandó y tórnome a mi menester. Con baja y enferma voz y inclinadas mis manos en los senos, puesto Dios ante mis ojos y la lengua en su nombre, comienzo a pedir pan por las puertas y casas más grandes que me parecía. Mas como yo este oficio le hobiese mamado en la leche (quiero

---

[7]Roland Barthes, *Système de la mode* (Paris, 1967), p. 278: " . . . on dirait que la Mode parle dans la mesure même où elle veut être système de signes." See also Petr Bogatyrev, "Costume as Sign," in *Semiotics of Art: Prague School Contributions*, eds. Ladislav Matejka and Irwin R. Titunik (Cambridge, Mass., 1976), pp. 13–19.

decir que con el gran maestro el ciego lo aprendí), tan suficiente discípulo salí, que aunque en este pueblo no había caridad ni el año fuese abundante, tan buena maña me di, que antes que el reloj diese las cuatro ya yo tenía otras tantas libras de pan ensiladas en el cuerpo, y más de otras dos en las mangas y senos (p. 139).

Lazarillo, like the squire, confronts Toledo with ritualized speech and behavior. Unlike his master, however, he gives words and receives food in return. The squire's pride and haughty manners contrast with Lazarillo's "baja y enferma voz," his "inclinadas . . . manos." The squire stands apart from the city "en una huerta," whereas Lazarillo walks from door to door and finally "por la Tripería" (*ibid.*) to beg their next meal. The "huerta" is a *locus amoenus* in which to play at love; the city is a place whose lack of charity—"no había caridad"—a much more vital love, is overcome not with the language of Ovid but with the speech of the blind beggar. The timeless quality of these "mañanicas de verano" during which lovers customarily gather at the river to "refrescar y almorzar" contrasts sharply with the two hours ("vi ser la dos. . . . antes que el reloj diese las cuatro") used so efficiently by Lazarillo. Survival in Toledo's economy does not permit the existence of fictional time or wasted words.[8]

If the shift in the relationship between Lazarillo and the *escudero* is detectable in a roundabout way through an analysis of their respective relationships to Toledo, no such indirect routes are necessary on our part to trace this shift as it develops in those scenes in which master and servant confront each other directly. The third *tratado*, more than any other, is filled with a linguistic confrontation in the form of dialogue. Lázaro recedes slightly into the background in order that Lazarillo and the squire may speak for themselves. Narrative is subordinated to speech, to direct address supplemented with Lazarillo's silent conversations with himself. These asides run counterpoint to the dialogue he shares with his master. Moreover, they are counter-balanced on the squire's part by silence, by his refusal to volunteer anything about his past until both he and Lazarillo know that each knows everything about the other's impoverished present. At that moment all secrecy ends. There are no more asides,[9] no more hidden thoughts, because master and servant function as equals in their shared

[8]Cf. Guillén, "La disposición," p. 275: "Las referencias cronológicas no son ya meros toques descriptivos. Constituyen la base del relato, el fondo contra el cual se dibuja la dilatación de un tiempo experimentado por Lazarillo."

[9]Douglas M. Carey, "Asides and Interiority in *Lazarillo de Tormes*," *SPh* 66 (1969): 120, notes that only one aside occurs in the final four chapters of the novel.

knowledge. But in the end it is Lazarillo who stands in a superior position. He has supported the squire with food and has protected his "honor" by remaining silent about his poverty. More importantly, however, the *escudero* fulfills Lazarillo's desire by breaking silence to narrate the history of his "valerosa persona" (p. 152): "Al fin se cumplió mi deseo, y supe lo que deseaba, porque un día que habíamos comido razonablemente y estaba algo contento, contóme su hacienda . . . " (p. 147). Ultimately, then, master yields to servant.

The struggle implicit within the confines of this nonreciprocal power semantic is more clearly evident in the choice of pronouns with which Lazarillo and the squire address each other. While they necessarily share in the dialogue, the squire is not allowed to hear his servant's silent speech contained in the asides. There are, then, two conversations.[10] The first is public, in that it defines the visible social relationship between master and servant. The second is private because Lazarillo's asides by their very nature do not allow the squire to speak and thus to have the conventional power and authority of master over servant. It must be emphasized, then, that Lazarillo's excessively familiar treatment of the squire (*tú*) exists only at the level of thought and not of speech. He thus reverses *silently* the pronoun of address with which the squire refers to him throughout the *tratado*. While the *escudero* speaks to Lazarillo as master to servant (pp. 130, 132, 133, 134, 135, 136, 140, 141, 145, 147, 148), Lazarillo responds with various modes of address, beginning with the relatively neutral *señor* (pp. 130, 132, 133, 134, 135, 140, 141, 146, 147, 148), soon introducing the respectful but more socio-linguistically significant *Vuestra Merced* (pp. 132, 135, 140), and ending with a much lower, almost denigrating *vos* (p. 148). Simultaneously he addresses the squire as his servant in his asides; *tú* is the pronoun of address throughout the *tratado* (pp. 132, 141 [two asides], 150). This allows the reader—the Vuestra Merced to whom the book is addressed, as well as ourselves—access to the squire's private truth, which stands behind his public fiction. More important for our purpose is the fact that the *tuteo* common to the voiced and unvoiced conversations of servant and master denotes a linguistic equality based on their shared poverty. It is only after Lazarillo realizes,

[10]We could label Lázaro's thought as "inner speech" and hence as "inner dialogue," according to V. N. Volosinov, *Marxism and the Philosophy of Language*, trans. Ladislav Matejka and Irwin R. Titunik (New York, 1973), p. 38: " . . . the units of which inner speech is constituted are certain *whole entities* somewhat resembling a passage of monologic speech or whole utterances. But most of all, they resemble the *alternating lines of a dialogue*."

for instance, that the squire intends to feed him with words that he begins his string of disparaging asides: " '¡Bien te he entendido!,' dije yo entre mí. '¡Maldita tanta medicina y bondad como aquestos mis amos que yo hallo hallan en la hambre!' " (p. 132). The unvoiced speech of Lazarillo's asides is diametrically opposed to the *verbum visibile* of honor that constitutes his master's fiction. By the end of the chapter the squire's secret poverty, which has been protected in the silence of Lazarillo's "mind," is forced into the open when the superior power of civil authority—represented in this case by the *alguacil* and *escribano*—requires Lazarillo to give a deposition of his master's assets. He repeats the squire's words and in so doing appropriates the language of the master while simultaneously establishing his own innocence as the victimized servant.

Only in silence, then, can Lazarillo be master in the presence of the squire; only in his thoughts can he address the squire with *tú*. There is, however, another pronoun of address—*vos*—that he speaks to his master and that communicates his disrespect and superiority. It is ironic that it is the squire who determines the pejorative value of *vos* within the chapter. Explaining his presence in Toledo as the result of "no más de por no quitar el bonete a un caballero su vecino" (p. 148), the squire reveals to what extent he refuses to be controlled by the protocol of gestural forms of address. He is an *escudero,* whose place in the social hierarchy is below that of a *caballero*[11] and who, according to the power structure of such a manorial system, must be submissive to the will of his superiors. He must initiate ritual greetings, taking the risk that he will be insulted with an inadequate or inappropriate response. Lazarillo pinponts hs master's untenable position within such a system when he abruptly asks: "—Señor—dije yo—, si él era lo que decís y tenía más que vos, ¿no errábades en no quitárselo primero, pues decís que él también os lo quitaba?" (*ibid.*). It is not that the squire refuses to remove his hat; rather he seeks to reverse the order of the gestural contract, to interrupt the process that is an integral part of the gesture itself. He answers his servant's question: "—Sí es, y sí tiene, y también me lo quitaba él a mí; mas, de cuantas veces yo se le quitaba primero, no fuera malo comedirse él alguna y ganarme por la mano—" (*ibid.*). He is so obsessed with the social power behind the act of doffing hats that his daily activities are motivated and controlled by his fear of being dishonored:

. . . si al conde topo en la calle y no me quita muy bien quitado del todo el

[11]Cf. Blecua, p. 149, n. 261.

bonete, que otra vez que venga me sepa yo entrar en una casa, fingiendo yo
en ella algún negocio, o atravesar otra calle, si la hay, antes que llegue a mí,
por no quitárselo (*ibid.*).[12]

This is the price he pays for being an "hombre de bien," subject to no
one, not even to the king "Que un hidalgo no debe a otro que a Dios y al
rey nada" (pp. 148–49).[13] Such an attitude precludes his integration
within the very system by which he is defined. The paralysis and
isolation that characterize his social position both in Valladolid and in
Toledo are self-induced because they are based on a value system that
is self-created. As Lazarillo pointed out earlier in the chapter, his own
"descontento" with his master stems from the squire's "presumpción"
and "fantasía" (p. 143). Both master and servant are searching for
masters, but the squire's pride rules out his being subservient to anyone
but himself, or the projected fiction of himself as an "hidalgo" and an
"hombre de bien."

Lazarillo's use of the pronoun *vos* to address the squire is not
innocent if we look at it in the context of his master's subsequent story,
in which he proudly claims to have dishonored an "oficial" in
Valladolid (p. 149). *Vos* takes on an explicitly pejorative connotation in
defining superior and inferior social relationships. Their verbal
encounter almost turns into physical violence:

Acuérdome que un día deshonré en mi tierra a un oficial, y quise ponerle
las manos porque cada vez que le topaba, me decía: "Mantenga Dios a
Vuestra Merced" "Vos, don villano ruin—le dije yo—, ¿por qué no sois bien
criado? ¿Manténgaos Dios, me habéis de decir, como si fuese quienquiera?"
De allí adelante, de aquí acullá me quitaba el bonete, y hablaba como debía
(*ibid.*).

The *oficial*, while recognizing the appropriate form of address, the
"Vuestra Merced," devalues it with the expression "Mantenga Dios.
. . . " There is no act of submission to the squire—visual or verbal—a
gesture which the squire demands because of his "high" rank.[14] He

[12]Antonio de Guevara, *Aviso de privados o despertador de cortesanos*, ed, A. Alvarez de la
Villa (Paris, n.d.) p. 127: "Si algún su igual, y aunque sea algo menor, viniere a hablar al
cortesano, es primor de crianza que hasta que se ponga la gorra no le debe dejar decir
palabras, porque es tan gran preeminencia hablar uno con otro la gorra quitada, que no
se sufre sino entre rey y vasallo y señor y siervo."

[13]Cf. Hermosilla, *Diálogo*, pp. 41–42: "Lorca. Pues, ¿cómo se entenderá lo que
algunos dicen: 'en quanto a hidalgo, no deuo nada al Rey'? Godoy. Vastará entender que
es dicho de necios, porque (en) ninguna nacion es tan a hidalgada como el Rey o Principe
della, ni tan libre; y si otros no lo dicen de mí por decirlo yo del Rey ni de otro, ¿qué abré
ganado o abentajado? Lorca. Muy rebuelto anda esto de vuestras hidalguias."

[14]Cf. Gatti, *Introducción*, p. 54: "La fórmula [Mantengaos Dios], palaciega en el siglo
XIV, era ya a fines del siglo XV, y más aún en el XVI, propia de los rústicos y de ahí la

attempts to reestablish his superiority by addressing the *oficial* as "vos," a pronoun that carries the same tone in virtually identical language in Jerónimo de Urrea's *Diálogo de la verdadera honra militar*.

> Jugando un día en Triana a basto y malilla con un escudero de don Pedro de Guzmán, llamado Belmar, le dixe, sin pensar enojallo: "Belmar, vos jugáis mal"; alterándose él por el vos que le dixe, respondió, empuñado y feroz: "Yo juego bien, y vos, que sois tú, sois muy ruin hombre."[15]

Even though the *oficial* as an *oficio* is immediately below an *escudero* in the social order, Lazarillo's master seeks to make the separation greater than it is by reconstituting the relationship through language. The *verbum visibile* of honor in the form of gestures and ritualized speech consists of the tipping of hats and proper speech behavior. Honor and language are synonymous for the squire; learning to speak a language is engaging in a rule-governing form of behavior within the institutional framework of honor, and Lazarillo, who up to this point in the novel stands outside all social institutions, is ignorant of its rules: "—Eres mochacho—me respondió—y no sientes las cosas de la honra, en que el día de hoy está todo el caudal de los hombres de bien" (p. 148). What Lazarillo does not understand is the language of honor, whose first rule is the subordination of others through speech. Thus the proper response, according to the squire, entails linguistic obeisance on the part of those who are inferior or who can be made inferior through verbal repression. They should say ("no les han de hablar menos de"), "Beso las manos de Vuestra Merced" or "Bésoos, señor, las manos" (p. 149), even though not literally following through with the act itself. The squire's speech comes to take the place of behavior, or rather, behavior exists only at the level of language within a system in which speech acts function as the basis of social interaction. If *vos* for the squire is a sign of social inequality, then Lazarillo's use of it to refer to his master points to a linguistic reversal of their original master-servant relationship. The *escudero* as a *Vuestra Merced* is reduced to *vos* by the end of an adventure in which beggar's language has overturned and subjected the *verbum visibile* of honor to a social system whose foundation is based on one's ability to feed oneself at the expense of others of higher rank. And the final scene in the third *tratado*

---

altiva actitud del puntilloso hidalgo." Also see María Rosa Lida de Malkiel, "Función del cuento popular en el *Lazarillo de Tormes*," in *Actas del primer congreso internacional de hispanistas*, ed, Frank Pierce and Cyril A. Jones (Oxford, 1964), pp. 349–59: " . . . Antonio de Guevara lamenta su sustitución por el beso (verbal) de manos o pie que pertenece exclusivamente al eclesiástico" (p. 357 and n).

[15]Venice, 1566. It is cited in José Pla Cárceles, "La evolución del tratamiento 'Vuestra-Merced,' " *RFE* 10 (1923): 245–80; the quotation is from p. 246.

definitively testifies to such a system.

The squire abandons his servant, leaving him to answer the demands of Toledo's judicial system with the same words with which he has made good his escape. But as Lazarillo discovered in the previous *tratado*, one does not live by words (bread) alone; however, it is possible to survive by appropriating someone else's words. When the *escribano* begins to take inventory of the squire's belongings, Lazarillo virtually repeats the fiction that the squire left behind:

> —Señores—dije yo—, lo que éste mi amo tiene, según él me dijo, es un muy buen solar de casas y un palomar derribado.
> —Bien está—dicen ellos—; por poco que eso valga, hay para nos entregar de la deuda. ¿Y a qué parte de la ciudad tiene eso?—me preguntaron.
> —En su tierra—les respondí.
> —Por Dios, que está bueno el negocio— dijeron ellos—, ¿y adónde es su tierra?
> —De Castilla la Vieja me dijo él que era—le dije yo.
> Riéronse mucho el alguacil y el escribano, diciendo:
> —Bastante relación es ésta para cobrar vuestra deuda, aunque mejor fuese (p. 154).

For all practical purposes, the squire's *solar* exists only at the level of language and, as such, is transferable wherever there are those who participate in the mimetic illusion of his language. Within Toledo's system, in which words are required to produce and to communicate more than fiction, saying that one is an "hombre de bien" is *only* language; it has no force. Thus each character turns to another for payment of services rendered. Words as currency do not satisfy the materialistic demands of service relationships:

> Y el alguacil y el escribano piden al hombre y a la mujer sus derechos. Sobre lo cual tuvieron gran contienda y ruido. Porque ellos alegaron no ser obligados a pagar, pues no había de qué ni se hacía el embargo. Los otros decían que habían dejado de ir a otro negocio que les importaba más por venir a aquél (p. 155).

Everyone's business is making money off the property of others; the old man and woman expect to collect the rent from the squire's estate; in turn, the constable and notary expect to be paid by the landlords for the inventory they could not carry out. The only *embargo* produced by their verbal battle is the "viejo alfamar de la vieja" (*ibid.*). Confiscated by a *porquerón*, it is forced to pay all debts despite its age and condition: " . . . creo yo que el pecador alfamar pagara por todos. Y bien se [le] empleaba, pues el tiempo que había de reposar y descansar de los trabajos pasados se andaba alquilando" (*ibid.*). Manipulating the

[43]

property of others for one's own benefit (profit) defines the economic foundation of Lázaro's "cumbre de toda buena fortuna" at the end of the novel. His taking advantage of the powerful influence of friends and marrying the archpriest's *criada* produce his good fortune and secure his control over all goods that are bought and sold in the city: " . . . el que ha de echar vino a vender, o algo, si Lázaro de Tormes no entiende en ello hacen cuenta de no sacar provecho" (p. 173).

These mutually dependent relationships between speech and production, honor and economy, commercial and manorial systems constitute a more profound text behind the third *tratado* we have been reading. They point to a fundamental dialectic between the *verbum visibile* of honor and Toledo's linguistic system as an economy. The squire's inability to sell his fiction is an indication of its lack of exchange value. There are no consumers who can "hear" his speech because Toledo's speech community as portrayed in the third *tratado* only responds to those messages that—as we will point out in our reading of the sixth *tratado*—are communicated through its economic vocabulary: *ganar, ahorrar, recaudar, comprar*. It is not that the community is unable to understand his language; rather it places no value on it as a mode of production and therefore provides no counterpart—no *co-locuteur*— with whom he can sustain a chain of honor-bestowing discourse. Verbal interchange for the community implies an exchange of money and services. This basic equilibrium in the squire's case is not established by the squire himself, who refuses to be contained within the service relationship that any conversation demands. Or to put it another way, he has priced himself out of Toledo's market by demanding more than anyone in the city is willing to pay. His honor and pride, based on birth and property within the manorial system, function as counterfeit currency in Toledo's linguistic marketplace, whose mode of operation can be expressed totally and concisely by the two most important verbs in the chapter: *trocar* and *negociar*. Exchange and trade are precisely the activities on which Lázaro will later build his *honra* and *provecho*.

# IV

αποσιωπησισ (*aposiopesis*): . . . cum intra nos supprimimus
ea, quae dicturi videmur, quod aut turpia aut invidiosa aut
alioqui nobis gravis dictu sunt. . . .

*Aquilae Romani*


. . . everyone hides the truth in matters of sex. . . .

Freud

One of the primary differences between the narration of the third *tratado* and that of the fourth is Lázaro's refusal in the latter to disclose the nature of his "whole" experience with the friar. As if anxious to proceed with his *Vida*, he terminates the narrative in the same abrupt way that he abandons his master: "Y por esto, y por otras cosillas que no digo salí dél" (p. 157). This self-censorship is especially curious when we recall that even his hidden thoughts regarding the *escudero* are communicated through the asides to Vuestra Merced. The fragmented narrative of the fourth *tratado* stands in opposition to the fully coherent narrative of the third. Lázaro's elliptical discourse is consciously produced by and directed toward the final silence at the end of the chapter. Speech, whether voiced or unvoiced, is no longer required to articulate the apparently unspeakable message that he chooses to suppress. No money or social status is at stake here; rather we encounter an inner, private experience, a sensitive phase of his life that—for reasons we intend to discover—he refuses to share. This screen of self-censorship, then, is drawn between Lázaro and ourselves, inviting us not only to determine its motivation but also to ascertain—however paradoxical it may seem—how his silence contributes to an understanding of the "entera noticia" of his "persona," to which he refers in the prologue.[1]

I have already argued that each of the previous *tratados* is concerned at one level with various initiations into new life situations, but more importantly, I have suggested how each can be seen as a distinct phase in Lazarillo's perception of the nature of language. From his awakening to metaphor (*tratado* 1) to his failure to manipulate it in an

---

[1] My purpose is to satisfy the frustrations of the reader as described by Lázaro Carreter, *Lazarillo*, p. 154: "El lector queda insatisfecho con que se le oculten las 'cosillas' que le ocurieron con el fraile. . . ."

extended fiction (*tratado* 2) to its value in establishing a space in society (*tratado* 3), he now arrives at a moment in which he discovers the communicating power of silence. He learns in what situations the voice is to be suppressed, when it no longer serves the function of verbalizing experience, and why it is desirable to maintain silence about certain matters that could be self-incriminating.[2] It is not surprising that Lázaro's concern for silence is precisely the key that links this chapter with the rest of the book. There is only one other place where he displays the same desire to suppress speech, and because he fails to do so, the narrative that we are reading is produced. His attempt to silence the gossip surrounding the behavior of his wife and the archpriest is directly related to his survival and the "cumbre de toda buena fortuna" he has attained as *pregonero* of Toledo:

> Hasta el dia de hoy nunca nadie nos oyó sobre el caso; antes, alguno siento que quiere decir algo della, le atajo y le digo:
> —Mirá, si sois amigo, no me digáis cosa con que me pese, que no tengo por mi amigo al que me hace pesar; ... Desta manera no me dicen nada y yo tengo paz en mi casa (pp. 176–77).

The "caso" to which he refers is of course the mutually beneficial arrangement between his final master—the archpriest—and himself. It is primarily a sexual liaison that, according to the slightly innocent words of evil gossipers, is expressed in terms of his wife's employment: " . . . veen a mi mujer irle a hacer la cama y guisalle de comer" (p. 175). Such sexual activity is not to be spoken of, or better, according to the archpriest, it is not to be listened to: "—Lázaro de Tormes, quien ha de mirar a dichos de malas lenguas nunca medrará" (*ibid.*). Self-imposed deafness will work as long as the wrong ears never hear and question the validity of the rumors. Silence, then, is the practical solution for the suppression of illicit sexual activity.

The interpretation of Lázaro's silence at the end of the fourth *tratado* must begin in the context of his attempt to establish silence at the end of the novel. It is not necessary, however, to equate both silences with sexuality only on the basis of these separate episodes. Within the fourth *tratado* itself, several references—both explicit and implicit—point to his adventure with the friar as being sexual in nature. It has been pointed out, for example, that the friar's "negocios seglares" (p. 156)

---

[2] Rico, "Problemas," p. 285, suggests that the fifth *tratado* "refuerza otra importante lección: la del callar y quedarse al margen cuando conviene, la del silencio en provecho propio. . . ." In the *fourth* tratado, we are clearly dealing with a different kind of silence, one in which Lázaro is directly involved.

and his "trote" (p. 157) refer to his role as a *trotaconventos*,[3] and the fact that he is a "fraile de la Merced," according to one interpretation, links him with the monastic order "que, en el Nuevo Mundo, presentaba un contraste escandaloso con las órdenes misioneras, por su falta de espíritu evangélico."[4] While these comments create an atmosphere within which the friar may have been perceived as scandalous in the sixteenth century, they do not build a step-by-step interpretation of the chapter itself; and more importantly for our analysis, they do not account for the fact that this episode is a censored experience in Lázaro's life.

The fourth *tratado* begins by looking back at the third, thereby establishing a continuity between the two chapters, and ends with a radical discontinuity, which is expressed through its abrupt silence. The *vecinas* who came to Lazarillo's defense as character witnesses also help him to find his next master: "Hube de buscar el cuarto, y éste fue un fraile de la Merced, que las mujercillas que digo me encaminaron" (p. 156). It is curious that they are no longer helpful neighbors. Rather they are renamed and thus redefined precisely because of their relationship with the friar, a relationship, it should be added, that is of a different order.[5] The friar in turn is also redefined by them as a *pariente*, a coded word that is, according to Alberto Blecua, sexually loaded.[6] This dualistic referential structure—*vecinas / mujercillas*, *fraile /pariente*—signals the underlying double discourse of the chapter. We immediately read that the friar is an *enemigo / amigo* ("gran enemigo del coro y de comer en el convento, perdido por andar fuera, amicísimo de negocios seglares y visitar" [*ibid.*]), that his *andar / trote* comprises his life, and that he consumes many more shoes ("más zapatos" [p. 157]) than does his servant ("primeros zapatos" [*ibid.*]). The end of the chapter is built on this same binary structure: "Y por esto, [what Lázaro has just narrated] y por otras cosillas que no digo [what he refuses to narrate] salí dél" (*ibid.*). This oscillation between saying and not saying exists at both the formally structural and the referential levels. It is indicative not of narrative indecision, but, on the contrary, of a narrative strategy that presents two discourses in a combinatory mode. In other words, we are presented with two stories,

[3] See Fred Abrams, "A Note on the Mercedarian Friar in the *Lazarillo de Tormes*," *RN* 11 (1969): 444–46.

[4] Bataillon, *Novedad*, p. 20.

[5] It is true that Lázaro refers to them as "mujercillas" earlier in the third *tratado* (p. 144); but it is their explicit association with the friar that later gives them a more pejorative, sexual function.

[6] Blecua, p. 157n.

the first (what Lázaro has just narrated) functioning as a screen for the other (that is, what he says he refuses to disclose). The sum of the elements of the screen story produces a coherent narrative but an irrelevant tale: Lazarillo meets a friar; they travel a great deal together, so much so that Lazarillo wears out a pair of shoes; for these reasons and for others omitted, he abandons his fourth master.

We are given a few elements that point to the meaning of this experience within the "entera noticia" of his life and help to flesh out the skeletal outlines described above. The friar maintains an unmonastic relationship to the world, but especially to women; his walking turns out to be of a special kind ("trote"); because of its frenetic nature and its direct connection with the first pair of shoes consumed by Lazarillo, his trade—simply referred to as "negocios seglares y visitar"—is to be interpreted at the level of the second discourse:

| 1. *vecinas* | *fraile* | *enemigo* | *andar* | *por esto* |
|---|---|---|---|---|
| 2. *mujercillas* | *pariente* | *amicísimo* | *trote* | *otras cosillas* |

The only other referent without an equivalence or contrast is the shoes. They are not given another name that would connect them to the second discourse and thus seem to belong solely to the first. They stand alone as the only non-oscillating signs in the narrative. Their primacy is further established by the fact that Lázaro sees them as representing a singularly iniciatory event. These are not ordinary shoes; they are extraordinary precisely because of their originary nature: "Este [the friar] me dio los *primeros* zapatos que rompí en mi vida" (*ibid.*, emphasis mine). The connection, then, between the friar's activities, Lazarillo's shoes, and the final silence of the chapter must be perceived as operating at the same level of discourse not only to disclose the source of self-censorship but also to suggest what the act of suppression means *sui generis*.

We are dealing in the fourth *tratado* with what Oswald Ducrot has called "tabous linguistiques," with one of those "thèmes entiers qui sont frappés d'interdit et protégés par une sorte de loi du silence (il y a des formes d'activité, des sentiments, des événements, dont on ne parle pas)."[7] Ducrot points out, however, that some situations may demand that such taboos be overcome or broken and that the speaker have at his disposal "des modes d'expression implicite, que permettent de laisser entendre sans encourir la responsabilité d'avoir dit."[8] Saying something prohibited but not accepting responsibility for having done

[7]*Dire et ne pas dire: Principes de sémantique linguistique* (Paris, 1972), p. 5.
[8]*Ibid.*, p. 6.

so requires a mode of discourse that is made to appear severed or disassociated from the speaker by the speaker himself. The strategy behind nonsaying is in itself a mode of saying. In other words, the speaker arranges his discourse in such a way that it speaks for itself. It is a free-floating discourse, unbound from the speaker by his utterances of denial ("otras cosas que no digo"), whose semantic signification rests solely on the ability of the *destinataire* to interpret properly the function of such a strategy. Lázaro finds himself in a difficult position. He is not called upon to report on the unmentionable behavior of the friar and someone else; rather his own behavior is at stake, and the way in which he presents it to Vuestra Merced will determine whether he too—like the *vecinas*, the *fraile*, and the friar's *negocios*—will be reinscribed at the level of the second discourse.

We must determine, however, if the elliptical discourse is what Ducrot calls "l'implicite de l'énoncé" or if it is "l'implicite fondé sur l'énonciation." Ducrot describes the first case: "Un procédé banal pour laisser entendre qu'on ne veut pas signaler de façon explicite, est de présenter à leur place d'autres faits que peuvent apparaître comme la cause ou la conséquence nécessaire des premiers."[9] In this case it is only the *destinataire*, "et non le locuteur," who is called on to "combler la lacune." In the second case the implicit "n'est plus à chercher au niveau de l'énoncé, comme un prolongement ou un complément du niveau explicite, mais à un niveau plus profond, comme une condition d'existence de l'acte d'énonciation."[10] The "implicite de l'énoncé" offers no interpretation; it is devoid of any level other than itself and its signification can only be provided by the *énoncé*. The "implicte fondé sur l'énonciation," however, contains another level, what Ducrot calls the *"sous entendus* du discours"[11] (our second discourse), which yields the necessarily obligatory interpretive keys. To put it another way, the abdication of responsibility for having communicated unspeakable messages exists only in the "implicite fondé sur l'énonciation," not at the level of the *énoncé* itself.

How does this refinement of the typology of the implicit help us to interpret the fourth *tratado*? First it exposes Lázaro's self-censorship as a strategy through which he discloses information while it simultaneously points to the fact that he "réduit sa responsabilité à la signification littérale"[12] of the discourse, declaring both his

9*Ibid.*, pp. 6–7.
10*Ibid.*, p. 9.
11*Ibid.*, p. 8.
12*Ibid.*, p. 12.

independence from it and his power over it. He confesses without saying that he is confessing. Moreover, we now see that the responsibility for the narration itself has been shifted to the level of the narrative, but even more important, it has been shifted to the *sous entendus* of the discourse. Not only does this displacement to the reinscribed referents in the text leave Lazarillo in innocent silence, but it signals a new awareness on his part of the ability and function of speech to communicate through its suppression.

How, then, do we have access to hidden communication? Let us return for a moment to the only objects that are not consciously transformed in the text: the shoes. Assuming that the second discourse tells a story about sexual experience and that silence elsewhere in the novel is concerned with the same subject, we can fill in some of the gaps by interpreting the incident of the shoes as a symbolic casting of Lazarillo's sexual initiation into life. Keeping in mind that elliptical discourse is a discourse of displacement, we can restate our problem in the following terms: "The pressure of the censorship has resulted in a displacement from a normal and serious association to a superficial and apparently absurd one."[13] This "normal and serious association" resides in the *sous entendus* of the discourse, and it is only by exploiting the bridges of association between the literal (the superficial) and the symbolic (the serious) that we will be able to reconstruct the pertinence of this *tratado* to the "entera noticia" of Lázaro's confessions. We have already detected the association between *vecinas* and *mujercillas*, *fraile* and *pariente*, and *andar* and *trote* and therefore can discard the first discourse and concentrate on the second. What we see is women of questionable morals ("mujercillas"), a friar of a particular kind ("de la Merced") whose business dealings relate him ("pariente") to the women,[14] and a boy who serves his master's business interests with great diligence. The only bridge between Lazarillo and the friar—except for the silence at the end of the chapter—is the shoes that are provided by Lazarillo's master, and as such, they are symbols of domination, power, and possession.[15] In this *tratado* it is Lazarillo who abandons his master, and not the other way around, as in the third chapter. But the act of giving Lazarillo the shoes is also an act of

[13]Sigmund Freud, *The Interpretation of Dreams*, in *The Standard Edition of the Complete Psychological Works of Sigmund Freud*, ed. and trans. James Strachey (with Anna Freud), 24 vols. (London, 1953–74). The citation is from vol. 5 (1953), p. 531.

[14]I am not referring to their function as *hilanderas*; that exists at the first level of discourse.

[15]See Jacob Nacht, "The Symbolism of the Shoe with Special Reference to Jewish Sources," *The Jewish Quarterly Review* 6 (1915–16): 1-22, esp. p. 2.

transfer. In other words, whatever is symbolized by the shoes is possessed by both master and servant. Moreover, the mode of possession is also the same because it is described with the same verb: ". . . pienso que *rompía* él más zapatos que todo el convento. Este me dio los primeros zapatos que *rompí* en mi vida" (pp. 156–57, emphasis mine). It is, then, the act of "breaking shoes" that equalizes the shared activities of Lazarillo and the friar.

There are, however, two fundamental differences in the way they share these experiences. First, the use of the imperfect tense to refer to the friar's shoes both indicates the quantity and habitual nature of his consumption and reveals him to be an experienced "shoebreaker." Second, the use of the preterite tense together with the singular qualifier ("primeros") points to Lazarillo's inexperience and emphasizes the newness and uniqueness, the introductory nature of the activity in his life. Neither the shoes nor Lazarillo could stand up to the pace and intensity: " . . . no me *duraron* ocho días ni yo pude con su trote *durar* más" (p. 157, emphasis mine). Both last the same amount of time and give out at the same moment. Lazarillo defines and is defined by the shoes. He is possessed by the shoes in the same way that he is dominated by the friar.

Thus far we have only elaborated the literal and consequently the superficial level of the relationship between master and servant. The power that the friar has over Lazarillo is not, however, the primary message contained by the shoe incident. It does not explain the motivation for the self-censorship; it only points to the function of the friar as the figure who makes available the experience itself. Having already suggested that silence is the result of repression and that silence and repression are associated in the novel at the level of sexuality, we can search for a more pertinent symbolism of the shoes. We can approach the shoes as a "dream idea"—to continue with Freud's terminology—which will lead us, through a process of association, to the meaning of the entire "dream." We should remind ourselves of the great dependence of the *Lazarillo* on folk literature, which recently was so convincingly demonstrated by Fernando Lázaro Carreter.[16] It may not be inappropriate, then, to turn to studies that have concentrated on the erotic symbolism of folktales, proverbs, fables, and even myths (classical and popular) to clarify the function of shoes in such narratives.

Dr. Aigremont's [Gotthilf Carl Siegmar, Baron von Schultze-

[16]*Lazarillo*, pp. 61–192; cf. Lida de Malkiel, "Función del cuento popular."

Galléra's] obscure and rare *Fuss-und Schuhsymbolik-und erotik*[17] rifles such texts and comes to the general conclusion that shoes have virtually always been associated with female genitalia. An equally pertinent conclusion, arrived at by obvious association, is that waking is symbolic of the sexual act itself. Wilhelm Stekel and Freud have suggested the same symbolic value of shoes in psychoanalysis.[18] But to return to texts, tales such as "Puss 'n Boots," "The Old Woman Who Lived in a Shoe," and "Cinderella," to name three of the most familiar, are centrally concerned with sexuality, marriage, and fertility. On a less popular level, we can consult Giovan Francesco Straparola's *Le piacevoli notti*,[19] in which "Madonna Modesta, moglie di messer Tristano Zanchetto, acquista nella sua gioventú con diversi amanti gran copia di scarpe." The number of shoes collected is explicitly related to the number of sexual favors granted:

> Aveva madonna Modesta per premio delle sue tante dolci fatiche e sudori omai empiuto un amplissimo magazzino di scarpe; ed eravi tanto grande il numero delle scarpe, e di ogni qualità, che chi fusse stato a Vinegia e cercato avesse ogni bottega, non arrebbe trovata la terza parte a comparazione di quelle che vi erano nel magazzino suo.[20]

In order to bring this brief but necessary detour back to our argument, one other piece of evidence should be mentioned because of its particular linguistic connection with our own text. "Breaking shoes" is a popular expression in French folk language whose specific sexual connotation is explained by Paul Sébillot: " . . . le terme 'avoir cassé son sabot' équivaut à: avoir perdu sa virginité."[21] The term "shoebreaking,"

---

[17]Leipzig, 1909; Wilhelm Stekel makes use of Aigremont in *Sexual Aberrations: The Phenomena of Fetishism in Relation to Sex*, trans. S. Parker, 2 vols. (New York, 1952).

[18]*Ibid.*, 1: 245, 366 n. 8; Freud, *Standard Edition*, 16: 348–49, 21: 152–57.

[19]ed. Giuseppe Rua. 2 vols. (Bari, 1927), vol.1, p. 247.

[20]*Ibid.*, p. 247.

[21]*Le folk-lore français*, 4 vols. (Paris, 1904), 1: 133. A folk poem from the Bohemian Forest of Germany also mentions shoebreaking, referring to childbirth: "Die Hültschuah wer(d)n brocha, / Sie Kimmit in d'Sechswocha" (cited in E. Hoffman-Krayer and Hanns Bächtold-Staubli, eds., *Handwörterbuch des deutschen Aberglaubens*, 10 vols. [Berlin and Leipzig, 1927–42], vol. 7, s.v. "Schuh," col. 1294). Cf. Arnold von Gennep, *Manuel de folklore français contemporain*, 4 vols. (Paris, 1937), vol. 1, pt. 1, p. 407: "Sans insister . . . sur le symbolisme du soulier comme signe de subordination, de vasselage et de transmission (*traditio*), on peut rappeler que, d'autre part, se laisser déchausser était pour une femme la marque d'un abandon aux désirs de l'homme, de la même manière que se laisser ôter le tablier ou dénouer la ceinture." I have not found a comparable shoe mythology in Spanish folklore. Cervantes, in *La gitanilla* (in *Novelas ejemplares*, ed. Francisco Rodríguez Marín, 2 vols. [1914; reprint ed., Madrid, 1962], 1: 19–20), has a *caballero* refer to Preciosa's metaphorical shoe in obviously sexual overtones: "Nadie te tocará a la vira de tu zapato; no, por el hábito que traigo en el pecho." Her honor will be defended with the

then, may be used to refer to sexual intercourse and its implications and, more specifically, to sexual initiation and loss of virginity, and thus there is no need to speak the prohibitive words. The lost connection between the shoe incident and the experience for which it stands is now apparent, but only at the symbolic level. And lest we be accused of imposing such a symbolic reading, we must now look for associations in the larger narrative.

Footwear as a symbol of sexuality is not limited to this *tratado* alone. [ |
There are two other references that, taken together with the *zapatos* in the fourth *tratado*, are able to confirm our reading. These are found at the beginning and at the end of the novel and function as a framework for chapter four. More important, however, all three taken together *in order* plot the sketchy outlines of Lazarillo's sexual life. The first occurs in the first *tratado*: "Y probósele cuanto digo y aun más porque a mí, con amenazas, me preguntaban, y como niño respondía y descubría cuanto sabía con miedo, hasta *ciertas herraduras* que por mandado de mi madre a un herrero vendí" (p. 94, emphasis mine). Lazarillo as a "niño" interprets the motivation for his stepfather's thievery as a stepson: that is, that he steals in order to fulfill his role as family provider: ("y con todo esto [the stolen goods] acudía a mi madre para criar a mi

honor of his military order. Rodríguez Marín cites the expression itself ("romper zapatos") in a proverb that in all probability intends poverty: "Zapato os daré que tengáis qué romper" (*12,600 refranes más, no contenidos en la colección del maestro Gonzalo Correas* [Madrid, 1930], p. 339). Several such proverbs were doubtless circulating in the middle of the sixteenth century as a result of the high cost and scarcity of shoes. Cf. *La premática que su Majestad ha mandado hacer este año de 1552 para remedio de la gran carestía que había en el calzado* (Alcalá de Henares). Rico, *La novela picaresca española*, p. xxxviii, sees a connection between Lazarillo, the *escudero*, and the "fraile de la Merced" through Sebastián de Horozco's "refrán glosado": "El mozo del escudero anda un año sin zapatos, después muele al zapatero." The interpretation of this *tratado* as one more elaboration of the theme of poverty would link it to the previous one(s) but would not, I think, account for the friar's shoes, Lazarillo's relationship to them, the sexual tone of the *tratado*, and Lázaro's final act of suppression.

Three final pieces of evidence are pertinent. Diego de Haedo's *Topographia e historia general de Argel* (Valladolid, 1612), describes the function of the shoe within an encoded sexual language: the unspeakable act represented by the positioning of the shoe communicates an unambiguous message. Haedo writes, "También es causa deshacer el matrimonio ser el marido con la mujer sodomita, como de ordinario lo son muchos, y en tal caso, cuando la mujer demanda justicia al cadí (que es el juez), sin hablar ni decir palabra, llegando delante del cadí toma su zapato y le pone delante dél con la suela para arriba, significando que el marido la conoce al revés, y es admitida a probanza" (fol. 35r). More contemporary in nature is the information communicated to me by my colleague, Louis Marin, who says that the French expression "trouver chaussures à son pied" means to find an appropriate wife (one who *fits*). And Beatriz Lavandera provides me with a Spanish expression from Buenos Aires, "tirar la chancleta" (*zapatilla*), which means to lose one's virginity or to have sexual intercourse; it also can mean simply to have a good time (*divertirse*).

[53]

hermanico" [*ibid.*]). From a less innocent viewpoint, however, the stepfather is seen to be sustaining an illicit sexual arrangement whose results have produced an illegitimate son. The nature of this relationship is discovered and brought to an end, not merely because Lazarillo tells all to the authorities, but because of the key item he includes in the confession. The horseshoes provide the missing connection between the rest of the stolen goods and Lazarillo's stepfather; they provide us with the key to an understanding of the narrative in which they occur. The circle of evidence is drawn closed when Lazarillo obeys his mother and sells the horseshoes and in so doing sells out his stepfather to justice. The horseshoes, then, are the symbols of the sexual exchange, it should be added, that originated in the Comendador's "caballerizas" (p. 93) and was nourished on thievery and silence.

We have already interpreted this episode (in chapter I) as a preview of the *caso* at the end of his life. It is not a coincidence that the other reference to footwear appears in the final *tratado*:

. . . tengo en mi señor arcipreste todo favor y ayuda, y siempre en el año le da en veces al pie de una carga de trigo; por las Pascuas, su carne; y cuando el par de los bodigos, las *calzas viejas* que deja (p. 174, emphasis mine).

Why these particular "gifts"? Whatever they may tell us about sixteenth-century society and history, their primary function is literary in nature and can be accounted for by the text itself. Again recalling our analysis in chapter I, we can see that the relationship between Lázaro, his wife, and the archpriest is—with obvious and important substitutions—a duplication of the relationship between Lazarillo, his mother, and Zaide. Both are based on economies of exchange: The archpriest (Zaide) provides Lázaro (Lazarillo) and his wife (mother) with material goods in exchange for continuing sexual favors. The wheat, meat, bread, and used stockings are not gifts at all, but the currency of exchange within their self-created system. The only items not related to Lázaro's physical sustenance are the stockings. They establish his identity as the archpriest's servant ("El vestido del criado dice quién es el amo"),[22] but more importantly, they constitute his livery

---

[22]Gonzalo Correas, *Vocabulario de refranes y frases proverbiales*, ed. Louis Combet (Bordeaux, 1967), p. 112a. Cf. Juan de Escobar, *Romancero del Cid*, ed. Carolina Michaelis Vasconcellos (Leipzig, 1875), p. 66: "Para salir, de contray / Sus escuderos vistió / Que el vestido del criado / Dice quien es el señor." Cf. also Blecua, pp. 174-75: "Era éste [calzas] regalo frecuente de amos a criados. . . ; no lo es tanto que estas calzas sean de un arcipreste—amancebado, además, con la mujer del criado—pues sin duda tenían un color especial que no podía pasar inadvertido a las gentes de Toledo."

of dishonor. The social value he places on clothing in general—learned from the *escudero* and later displayed after serving the *capellán*—reveals his vulnerability to a nonverbal sign system (the *verbum visible* of honor), a silent but powerful language that communicates the truth concerning his arrangement with the archpriest. The stockings, then, along with the shoes and horseshoes, form the vocabulary of a repressed sexual language, whose force bridges the silence of self-censorship to communicate through a symbolic discourse. The fact that these particular stockings are used by the archpriest further underscores their complicit arrangement, but more pertinently, it focuses attention on the archpriest as the sexual perpetrator. In one sense his giving the stockings to Lázaro is simply restoring them to their proper owner. After all, he has been using them to wear his servant's shoes (wife).

The symbolic discourse on footwear also contains a narrative. Lazarillo's completely innocent introduction to sexuality is expressed in the novel through the animallike shoes of his parents. He is not aware of the true content of the confession he gives to the authorities. In his adventure with the friar, however, the fact that he suppresses his biography indicates that he is well aware of what he refuses to tell Vuestra Merced. And at the end of his *Vida*, as an adult, he admits both explicitly and implicitly not only the role that sexuality plays in life but also his manipulation of it for his own advantage. We are dealing with a narrative that moves from the unconscious through a stage of suppressed consciousness to a final, total articulation of a very private sexual biography. This series of transformations and displacements is, of course, central to an overall narrative strategy in which he seeks to claim at the end a new innocence by shifting the responsibility for his final sexual situation—the *caso*—to the archpriest. He presents the mask of an obedient servant who has followed the orders of his master in order to gain his good will: "Y visto por mí que de tal persona no podía venir sino bien y favor, acordé de lo hacer [marry his "criada"]. Y así, me casé con ella, y hasta agora no estoy arrepentido. . . . Y hízonos alquilar una casilla par de la suya" (pp. 174–75). At the moment that he tells his story he is the servant of Vuestra Merced.

The fourth *tratado* plays an integral part from the beginning to the end of his autobiography; that is, it functions as the central link in the chain of symbols of the implicit: *herraduras-zapatos-calzas*. As the "dream idea," it brings together by association the friar's "negocios" and Lazarillo's hidden sexual initiation. The "fraile de la Merced" is, then, a "pariente" / *trotaconventos* whose designated public role as the charitable rescuer of Christian captives is literally that of a liberator of prisoners of love.[23] His "mujercillas" are to be equated with the number of *zapatos* he consumes. In sum, he is Lazarillo's master and sexual mentor.

The friar provides Lazarillo with the first shoes (woman) that he "breaks," but his status as "pariente," to return momentarily to the description of the *mujercillas*, suggests—and only suggests—an even more secret and more nefarious mode of existence. While he may be related to them because of his "negocios seglares," he may have another type of *parentesco*, namely, of gender. Alberto Blecua points out that family relationships constitute a code and reveal something quite other than what they seem to indicate, especially when no blood ties are concerned. His evidence is worth repeating. He quotes Villalobos, *Algunas obras*: " . . . debe haber veinte años bienaventurados que ella es manceba de un clérigo bien honrado y gordo, el cual (santa gloria haya) la llamaba sobrina" (p. 157, n. 287). The connection between the two words (other than the explicitly stated one) is their gender, indicated by the nature of language itself: *manceba / sobrina*. The relationship *fraile / pariente*, however, denotes a sexual transformation. He is genderless. He is not "padre," "amigo," or even the euphemistic "sobrino," for all of these would identify his maleness. The insinuating *mujercillas*, like the secret *cosillas* at the end of the *tratado*, alludes to a silence that results from a self-censorship of a delirious nature, which, in Freud's words, "no longer takes the trouble to conceal its operation; instead of collaborating in producing a new version that shall be unobjectionable, it ruthlessly deletes whatever it disapproves of, so that what remains becomes quite disconnected."[24] The new version of which Freud speaks is in the fourth *tratado* Lázaro's heterosexual experience as cast at the level of symbolic discourse. That ruthless deletion is, of course, of the "otras cosillas," and it discloses their inability to be contained even in symbols.

Is there, then, no accessibility to the silence that lies beyond symbolic discourse? That is, is it possible to further refine Ducrot's typology of the implicit to speak of the nature of the "condition d'existence de l'acte d'énonciation" rather than of the act itself? Pursuing such a course takes us away from both the literal, transparent discourse and the symbolic discourse, with which we have been concerned, and directs us instead to silence as the source of signification. To put it another way, "l'acte d'énonciation" moves to the foreground as the *énoncé* of the text.

[23]Cf. Abrams, "Note"; and Blecua, p. 157: "Lázaro sería rescatado de su 'cautiverio', irónicamente, por un fraile de la Merced."

[24]Freud, *The Interpretation of Dreams*, p. 529.

The act of not speaking and the secret to which it refers ("otras cosillas que no digo") have replaced the text ("por esto"), which to this moment has functioned as the mediator between Lázaro and Vuestra Merced. This relaxation of the tension between the *énonciation* and the *énoncé* is illusory, however, because in its place a far greater tension surfaces. There is no discourse behind which Lázaro can play hide-and-seek; there is only the secret, the sexual taboo, whose nature would condemn him by association.

Lázaro's desire to communicate the "entera noticia" of himself is expressed in terms of his refusal to communicate. Yet the act of a negative *énonciation* (silence), because of its conscious sabotage of the communicating function of language, invites an interpretation. It is not by chance that in the act of abolishing speech, he also rids himself of the friar, for both point to transgressions of equal consequence. Language and sexuality are put on the same plane and are treated as silence-inducing activities. This turning about, or inversion, at the level of speech is simply the *perversio* of rhetorical discourse ("Transgressio est quae verborum perturbat ordinem perversione aut transiectione" [*Rhetorica ad Herennium* 4. 32. 44]) confined in a strict sense to the disturbance of "normal" word order.[25] In a wider sense, however, it is condemned because of its possible defective influence on the clarity and structure of artistic composition, whose main function is to make "omnes partes orationis aequabiliter perpolitas" (*ibid.*, 4. 12. 18). Is it possible to establish a link between (1) the *perversio* of rhetorical discourse and the proper construction of artistic composition and (2) the interrupting "acte d'énonciation" and the friar's effect on Lázaro's confession? Yes, but only if we conceive of the truncated narrative of the fourth *tratado* as a complete *énoncé*, that is, as one that communicates a full but unspeakable event. The secret experience with the friar functions as a form of *perversio* because it results in the transgression of the established process of the communicating voice. The friar's perversion is to be interpreted, not at the level of Lazarillo's experience as his servant, but at the level at which he perversely affects the linguistic reconstitution of that experience. His sexually perverse life is contained in the same silence—the repression of those "cosillas"—with which Lázaro suppresses and closes his narrative. The communication of his heterosexual initiation into life is realized through the diversion of the text from *énoncé* to *énonciation* and from a

25Lausberg, *Manual*, 2: 161–62.

literal to a symbolic discourse, whose interpretation depends on the sexualized *zapatos* and their central place within the *herraduras-zapatos-calzas* chain. The secret crime to which Lázaro refers—the friar's homosexuality[26]—remains at the level of implicit communication, permitting only an interpretation based on insinuation ("pariente") and its effects, not on the "acte d'énonciation," but on the existing condition that motivates it. The movement from a textual diversion to a textual perversion is contained in the movement from a symbolic discourse to silence.

While Lázaro's act of suppression reveals his power of implicit communication, it simultaneously signals his vulnerability to the voices of others. He silences his own voice to hide a past sexual experience but later is unable to effect the same result when confronted by the active gossip of his neighbors in Toledo. His recourse is to stabilize his voice through a new mode of communication—writing—whose potential he discovers while serving the *buldero*, in the fifth *tratado*.

[26]Márquez Villanueva, "La actitud espiritual," p. 79; Molho, *Romans picaresques espagnols*, p. xxix. Homosexuality was of course the unspeakable crime; cf. Lactantius, *Divinarum Institutionum*, bk. 6, chap. 23: "Non potest haec res pro magnitudne scleris enarrari," in *Opera omnia*, ed. Samuel Brandt (Prague, 1890).

V

Quum potestas conferendi indulgentias a Christo Ecclesiae concessa sit, atque hujusmodi potestate divinitus sibi tradita antiquissima etiam temporibus illa usa fuerit.

*Sacrosancti et ecumenici Concilii Tridentini . . . canones et decreta*

L'écriture porte la mort.

*Jacques Derrida*

he fourth *tratado* concludes Lazarillo's introduction to the fullest possibilities of the communicating power of speech. He and the friar do not speak to each other. Much of their experience together is carried on in silence, but it is a silence that communicates the hidden nature of their relationship. Lázaro's elliptical discourse, his refusal to complete those silent gaps with words, signals the end of the portion of his life that began with his discovery of voice and concludes with its suppression. If withholding language but not truth is characteristic of the fourth *tratado*, then the fifth can be viewed as a reversal of this relationship, for it demonstrates how full disclosure through full discourse can be manipulated for purposes of deception. The conspiracy invented by the pardoner and the constable depends and is built on the ability of language to communicate truth; paradoxically, the fraudulent *buldero* must be accepted as a fraud so that his congregation will buy his *bulas*.

More important from the viewpoint of how this *tratado* contributes to the novel's linguistic interests is the fact that for the first time, a text—written language—comes into explicit contact with speech. It is the relationship between them that interests the author of the *Lazarillo*. The bull must be preached; it must be presented with oral language so that it can be sold. By the end of the *tratado* a change has taken place that points to the virtually unlimited power of speech to constitute reality. The pardoner's rhetoric has created a space in which the bull speaks in its own behalf, as it were, free from the *buldero*'s intervention: " . . . en diez o doce lugares de aquellos alderredores donde fuimos, echó el señor mi amo otras tantas mil bulas *sin predicar sermón*" (p. 165, emphasis mine). The bull as a mode of *écriture* has silenced the voice of the pardoner and stands independently as a sacred text of unquestionable validity and authority. It has become truth and can be bought by a knowing but (somehow) simultaneously "inocente gente" (p. 169).[1] On a more basic level, the bull provides the pardoner an ever increasing income a secure investment as long as he maintains its linguistically bestowed efficacy.

The *bula* however, does not function only as a papal indulgence[2] that is, as a sixteenth-century *bula de la cruzada*. Because of its special status as the only text within the *Lazarillo,* I will propose that it is an analogue (*analogia*)[3] of the novel and that the way in which it is "sold" to its audience is analogous to the way in which Lázaro directs his *Vida* to Vuestra Merced. Moreover, this internal relationship between writer and reader in turn points to the external relationship between the anonymous author and his readers. In sum, the author of the *Lazarillo* constructs the fifth *tratado* in such a way as to reveal the strategy of the entire book. But before we are able to say something about the larger

[1] Jacques Derrida, *De la grammatologie* (Paris, 1967), p. 174, expresses in current critical thought the exact process that occurs in the fifth *tratado*: "Seule une communauté innocente, seule une communauté de dimensions réduites . . . . seule une micro-société de non-violence et de franchise dont tous les membres peuvent droitement se tenir à portée d'allocution immédiate et transparente, 'cristalline', pleinement présente à soi dans sa parole vive, seule une telle communauté peut subir, comme la surprise d'une aggression venant *du dehors*, l'insinuation de l'écriture, l'infiltration de sa 'ruse' et de sa 'perfidie'. Seule une telle communauté peut importer de *l'étranger*."

[2] I am aware of the distinction that Márquez Villanueva, "La actitud espiritual," draws between *bulas* and *indulgencias* (p. 75n), and I also have in mind García de la Concha "La intención religiosa," p. 269, where he says " . . . me parece una sutileza innecesaria." The distinction is very necessary in my argument, and thus I do not treat them synonymously, but in the way indicated by the Alcalá interpolator: " . . . y para que se supiese quién eran los que habían de gozar de la sancta indulgencia y perdones de la sancta bula. . ." (Blecua, p. 166). Cf. Alejo Venegas, *Agonía del tránsito de la muerte* (Alcalá de Henares, 1565):" . . . bulla no es la indulgencia ni el papel en que se escriue, sino el sello de plomo que viene pendiente d'la bulla; tómase el sello por la misma indulgencia" (cited in Gili Gaya, *Tesoro lexicográfico,* s.v. "bulla"). The conventional relationship between them is described concisely in the *Dictionnaire de théologie catholique* (Paris, 1923), Vol. 2, pt. 1, s.v. "bulle": "Leur object comprend: les décisions doctrinales; les sentences de canonisation; la discipline ecclésiastique; les jubilés; *la promulgation d'indulgences génerales*. . . ." To put it another way, in the linguistic terms we have been using, the bull as a piece of paper is the sign; the indulgence, the signified. In buying the bull, the pardoner will argue (as did the Church), one simultaneously acquires its power (indulgence). In this *tratado*, as we will see, the townsfolk are convinced, not by its power over purgatory, but by its power over the reality of the present when it appears to heal the constable.

[3] Quintilian, *Institutio oratoria,* ed. and trans. H. E. Butler, Loeb Classical Library, 4 vols. (London, 1920–22), 1:112: "Eius [analogiae] haec vis est, ut id quod dubium est ad aliquid simile, de quo non quaeritur, referat et incerta certis probet." Lausberg's comment is pertinent (*Manual*, 2: 18): "La *analogia* es, pues, un *argumentum a simili*. . . aplicado al lenguaje; y presupone que el lenguaje posee una estructura completamente semejante. . . ." I am of course, comparing not words but structures: the known structure of the pardoner's strategy with the unknown structure of Lázaro's strategy.

problem of anonymity and language, we must first discover the *bula*'s function within the narrative, that is, within Lazarillo's growth toward his final position in the novel as town crier, because it is only through such an analysis that the bull as analogue is admissable as part of Lázaro's strategy to seduce Vuestra Merced into his text.[4]

It is clear from the beginning of the *tratado* that the pardoner is a wretched character. He is not just ordinarily wretched; Lázaro emphasizes the fact that he is the most shameless of all the *quaestuarii* he has met or hopes to meet: ". . . el más desenvuelto y desvergonzado, y el mayor echador dellas [bulas] que jamás yo vi ni ver espero, ni pienso que nadie vio" (p. 158). There is no doubt as to where Lázaro stands in relation to his fifth master. He separates himself completely from the "modos y maneras y muy sotiles invenciones" (*ibid.*) that the pardoner employs to deceive the ignorant populace. To make this distance as great as possible and yet to remain "present" Lázaro quickly discards the use of the first-person pronoun, using it again only in the final sentence.[5] The *yo* does not disappear altogether, however, for it is used by both the pardoner and the constable in their respective performances before the congregation. The effect of this pronoun shift is obvious but crucial: Lázaro's role as mediator (narrator) moves into the background, thus allowing a virtually unmediated narrative relationship to exist between Vuestra Merced and the characters in the story that Lázaro is telling. And where is Lazarillo? He is found among the crowds, observing with them while simultaneously maintaining his proper servant status to his master: "Y así quedó mi amo muy enojado. Y después que los huéspedes y vecinos le hubieron rogado que perdiese el enojo, y se fuese a dormir, se fue, y así nos echamos todos" (p. 160).

There is no hint that the argument between the constable and Lazarillo's master is staged. Lazarillo is as duped as the rest because it is only at the end that he realizes their complicity: ". . . con ver después la

[4]This text is not so much the literal text that we hold in our hands as it is the cultural text established by Lázaro's language on the one hand and the documentary nature of the pardoner's indulgences on the other. Cf. Maurice Merleau-Ponty, *Signs*, trans. Richard McCleary (Evanston, 1964), pp. 96–97: "Ideal existence is based upon the document. Not, undoubtedly, upon the document as a physical object, or even as the vehicle of one-to-one significations assigned to it by the language it is written in. But ideal existence is based upon the document insofar as . . . the document solicits and brings together all knowing lives—and as such establishes and re-establishes a 'Logos' of the cultural world." The bull as a document is the first motivation for bringing together the populace of Sagra de Toledo.

[5]Raymond S. Willis, "Lazarillo and the Pardoner: The Artistic Necessity of the Fifth *Tractado*," *HR* 27 (1959): 267–79, esp. pp. 274–77.

risa y burla que mi amo y el alguacil llevaban y hacían del negocio, conoscí cómo había sido industriado por el industriado y inventivo de mi amo" (p. 165). Without Lázaro's explicitly directing hand, Vuestra Merced is put in the place of Lazarillo, for his discovery of the truth of the conspiracy is simultaneous with Lazarillo's. Vuestra Merced, then, is made part of the text not only as its receiver; he becomes part of that "inocente gente" within the text. Lázaro has seduced him with his own *sotil invención* by playing the role of a metaphoric *buldero*. Finally, to carry the analogy one step further, Lázaro succeeds in "selling" this chapter in the same way that he "sells" his autobiography: In spite of the fact that it confesses the truthful nature of the evil rumors about himself—that he is no more saintly than his neighbors, that is, that he is as "desenvuelto and desvergonzado" as the *buldero*—his text stands independent of his sordid behavior in order to guarantee his status as town crier and as author.

The complicity between the pardoner and the constable is also the complicity between Lázaro and his story. Chapter five explores the mechanism of narrative complicity within a story that is based on complicity. At the root of such a relationship is an act of withholding, an elliptical discourse whose silent gaps contain the necessary information to communicate the whole truth. In this case, however, it is not that the crucial bit of data is masked by silence but rather that it is deferred until the proper moment for disclosure. Such a project assumes absolute mastery of the art of persuasion—of forensic oratory—to move one's audience to action: in this case to buy the *bulas*. Moreover, it requires an ability to invent carefully structured fictions that are based on a series of cues designed to elicit audience response *at desired moments*. The complexities inherent in such verbal orchestration are revealed by the pardoner and his rhetoric. It is not surprising, then, that Lázaro introduces him as a preacher, a sophisticated rhetorician, whose artistry extends well beyond his legitimate space behind a pulpit. The entire world is his "congregation," and the fiction he creates to sell his *bulas* is his "sermon."

There are, then, two rhetorical discourses at the level of the narrative in this *tratado*. The first is concerned with the pardoner's efforts outside the doors of the church to manipulate the population of Sagra de Toledo. The second is specifically related to the sermon that he preaches from behind the pulpit. Both are integrally connected because his successful persuasion of the skeptical audience in the church is directly based on his success in blinding the community at large. But before I discuss the interdependency of both discourses, a brief digression into the history of the *quaestuarii* and their merchandise is necessary in order to recover the context in which a sixteenth-century Vuestra Merced could have viewed the *buldero* that Lázaro places before him.

It has been argued persuasively that the *buldero* of the fifth *tratado* may have stepped out of the pages of Masuccio's *Il Novellino*.[6] That he shares certain characteristics with those clerical tricksters who populated works of a semipopular nature—the *Speculum cerretanorum* or various texts in the *Liber vagatorum* tradition, for instance—is indisputable.[7] But it is also true that the *quaestuarii* were very much a part of the daily life of the time,[8] especially in sixteenth-century Spain, "where the effects of the Counter-Reformation were scarcely felt, long after they had become dominant throughout the other lands of the Roman obedience."[9] Various kinds of papal bulls were allowed in Spain, but the most popular (and most lucrative) of these was the *Bula de la Santa Cruzada*, whose yearly "profits" during three years (1551–54) totaled more than 755,000 ducats.[10] By the end of the century (1584), the Venetian envoy to Spain, Vincenzo Gradenigo, estimated that the indulgences of the Crusade were producing around 600,000 ducats per year.[11] Most of the revenue went into the royal treasury, but approximately 20,000 ducats per year went to the Church.[12] Even if these figures are grossly exaggerated, the two *reales* paid for each bull gives a rough idea of the number that were sold every year.[13]

[6]See Joseph V. Ricapito, "*Lazarillo de Tormes* (Chapter V) and Masuccio's Fourth *Novella*," *RPh* 23 (1970): 305–11; and Rico, *La novela picaresca españolas*, p. xl: "Haya influjo concreto de Masuccio o no lo haya, lo cierto es que el ardid del buldero constituía casi un tópico literario."

[7]Joseph E. Gillet, "A Note on the *Lazarillo de Tormes*," *MLN* 55 (1940): 130–34, argues that a Flemish version of the *Liber vagatorum* is a "likely source" (p. 132).

[8]José Goñi Gaztambide, "Los cuestores en España y la regalía de indulgencias," *Hispania Sacra* 2 (1949): 3–45, 285–310, esp. pp. 26–43 ("Abusos de los cuestores en la época del Concilio de Trento"); see also *idem, Historia de la Bula de la Cruzada en España* (Vitoria, 1958).

[9]Henry Charles Lea, "Indulgences in Spain," *Papers of the American Society of Church History* (1889): 129. The following summary is based on this study and on *idem, History*; on Goñi Gaztambide, "Los cuestores" and *Historia*; and on Aristide Rumeau, "Notes au *Lazarillo; 'Despedir la bula,'* " *LNL* 163 (1962): 2–7.

[10]Goñi Gaztambide, *Historia*, p. 507: "Si a esta cantidad se añaden los ingresos obtenidos en Sicilia, Cerdeña y Canarias, y las composiciones, resultará un producto líquido a favor del tesoro real de 972.466 ducados. . . ."

[11]Lea, *History*, p. 429.

[12]Goñi Gaztambide, *Historia*, p. 488.

[13]*Ibid.*, p. 503: "La limosna mínima que había que entregar era de dos reales. Despachábanse buletas en tanto número, que las imprentas de San Pedro Mártir de

From a purely economic viewpoint, these pieces of paper became more valuable than money.[14] Thus the printing offices in Spain were heavily guarded. According to Henry Lea,

> the printing office had its windows filled with heavy iron grilles, covered with copper net-work; the door was locked with two keys, each entrusted to a friar, both of whom had to be present when any one entered or departed, or when food was introduced, and all who passed the door were searched, on going in for white paper and on coming out for printed bulls. Every sheet of paper was numbered when delivered to the printer, and was accounted for and registered when printed.[15]

Such protective custody bespeaks massive fraud and theft, and although the efficacy of stolen "official" bulls supposedly evaporated, there was a ready market for their disposal. Since the pardoners were paid on a commission basis, the more they sold, the more they earned.[16] Again from this economic viewpoint, the more persuasive salesmen had access to a potentially unlimited source of income. Their concern for the spiritual well-being of their congregations was reinforced, as it were, according to the degree of their own greed. Steadily increasing reports of abuses throughout the century, as reflected in the promulgated laws against unscrupulous and avaricious pardoners, suggest that they were greedy indeed. In 1348, 1380, 1472, 1512, and 1525 (Toledo) the Cortes of Castile complained of the methods used by the pardoners to distribute their wares.[17] In 1524 Charles V issued a *pragmática*

> forbidding the preachers and treasurers from interfering unnecessarily with the labors of the people, from punishing them for non-attendance at the sermons, from compelling them to take the bulls against their will, or oppressing them in any manner, from forcing them to go beyond the bounds of their towns or parishes in accompanying the bull on its arrival

Toledo, P. P., y la de nuestra Señora del Prado de Valladolid, que desde 1501 tenían el monopolio de impresión, apenas podían dar abasto."

[14]*Idem*, "Los cuestores," p. 27: "Las Buletas de monasterios y hospitales predicadas por el Consejo de Cruzada en favor de la guerra contra los infieles eran tratadas como mercancía. Según se informó en 1543 el embajador Juan de Vega, genoveses y otros mercaderes las compraban por 800 ducados y las revendían a los tesoreros de la Cruzada por 2.000."

[15]Lea, "Indulgences," p. 157.

[16]Rico, *La novela picaresca española*, pp. xli–xlii: " . . . alquilaban [los mercaderes] predicadores especializados, quienes a su vez recibían un tanto por bula: semejante confluencia de intereses privados es lo que originaba la mayoría de 'desafueros.' " Cf. Goñi Gaztambide, *Historia*, p. 367.

[17]Cf. Margarita Morreale, "Reflejos de la vida española en el *Lazarillo*," *Clavileño* 30 (1954): 28–31.

and departure—all of which shows the ingenuity with which the sale was extended.[18]

In 1528 and 1554 this law was renewed; in 1601 Philip III reiterated the abuses mentioned earlier.

These abuses were mere inconveniences compared with the methods used to collect payments for those bulls purchased on forty-day credit. The responsibility for obtaining the money lay with the town council (*concejo*), for it had to account financially for all bulls sold by the pardoner but not paid for at the time of purchase. The council appointed a collector (*cogedor*) to enforce its authority "por todo rigor de Derecho," according to a *pragmática* of May 1554. It is worth reproducing part of this royal decree not only to understand more fully the nature of the procedure but also to have an idea of how far the council could go in exercising its power:

> . . . que dentro de quarenta dias, despues de pasado el plazo a que las dichas Bulas se hubieren de pagar, dará cobrados los maravedís, que montaren las Bulas que se le entregaren al dicho Tesorero, o a quien su poder hubiere, llanamente sin pleyto alguno; porque al tiempo que se le entregaren el padrón y Bulas, se ha de averiguar ante la Justicia del tal lugar, en presencia del dicho cogedor, si hay algunas personas de las contenidas en el dicho padrón de quien no se pueda cobrar, por pobres, o escritos dos veces, o no poder ser habidos los que las deben: y que si al plazo susodicho no diere cobrados los dichos maravedís al dicho Tesorero, o a quien su poder hubiere, que la persona que en nombre del dicho Tesorero los fuere a cobrar del, lo execute por todo rigor de Derecho; lo qual execute solamente por virtud de la obligación, o cedula que el tal cogedor hubiere hecho de las Bulas que hubiere rescebido; que para ello, y traer vara de nuestra Justicia, le damos poder cumplido, llevando poder del dicho Tesorero, y aprobacion del Gobernador o Corregidor; o Justicia de la cabeza de cada diocesi y partido: y asimismo damos poder y facultad al cogedor que fuere nombrado por los dichos Consejos, para que pueda compeler y apremiar a todas las personas que debieren las dichas Bulas, a que se las den, y paguen pasado el término a que se hubieren dado fiadas; y sobre ello hagan las execuciones, ventas y remates de bienes necesarios, como por maravedís del nuestro haber, con que no puedan llevar, ni sacar prendas algunas de un lugar a otro, si no fuere a la cabeza de la jurisdiccion, no hallando comprador en el lugar donde se tomare. . . .[19]

There were, then, various attempts to halt the questionable methods that the *quaestuarii* used to distribute their bulls. But simultaneously

[18]Lea, "Indulgences," p. 162.
[19]Novísima recopilación de las leyes de España, 6 vols. (Madrid, 1805–7), vol. 2, p. 297.

royal decrees were promulgated that seemed to spur them on by giving civil authorities virtually unlimited powers to extract payment for those same bulls. The pardoners' responsibilities ended at the point when their victims *agreed* to purchase the *bulas*. Property was confiscated to cover debts and delinquent accounts, and any money left over from ensuing auctions was returned to the former owners.[20] Taking care of one's spiritual welfare had potentially disastrous financial—and physical—consequences. It is no wonder that the victims of such a system were reluctant to attend sermons or unwilling to purchase bulls. Yet thousands were sold every year. How is this to be explained?

Aside from the threat of excommunication for refusing to buy them,[21] there were other, more positive reasons for obtaining as many as possible. The *bula* was a form of after-life insurance, and the piece of paper on which it was printed was a policy. Long before the sixteenth century it was popularly thought that bulls could pardon *a culpa et a poena*, a remission of sin that went well beyond the "penance" that they were intended to mitigate. Contrition and confession were prerequisites for their efficacy. However, these were conveniently forgotten by the beginning of the sixteenth century. "Erasmus," as Lea writes, "evidently was guilty of no exaggeration when he described the wicked as tossing from their evil gains a coin for an indulgence, and then, thinking their sins all wiped out, engaging in fresh ones."[22] The seemingly miraculous power of bulls was believed in to such an extent that they were bought after sins were committed in expectation of remission. They were also thought to make sins less sinful. Azpilcueta, for instance, argued later in the century that

> the man who sins in the expectation of remission is not more guilty but less, for he who sins without hope of pardon comes near to being a despairing sinner, and is therefore more wicked, while he who sins in the hope of pardon mitigates the gravity of his sin.[23]

The power of bulls extended to the dead as well as to the living. For two *reales* a bull could be purchased to alleviate the suffering of those who had already died.[24] Alonso Pérez de Lara's *Compendio de las tres gracias de*

---

[20]Goñi Gaztambide, *Historia*, p. 513: " . . . merecían mayor indignación los atropellos de los receptores con los pobres que no disponian de dinero contante en el momento de tomar la bula, a los que sacaban prendas vendiéndolas después a precio vil por menos de lo que valian o les fiaban las bulas para llevarles despúes al tiempo del pago 'hasta las sábanas de la cama.' "

[21]*Ibid.*, p. 509.

[22]Lea, *History*, p. 76.

[23]*Ibid.*, p. 83.

[24]This was a widespread, popular belief: "En vano protestó fray Juan de Argomanas,

*la Santa Cruzada* (Madrid, 1610), although written long after the publication of the *Lazarillo*, tends to reflect especially the practical aspects involved in the sale and distribution of bulls during the reign of Philip II. Composed as a kind of "working guide for officials employed in the *Cruzada*,"[25] it contains a sample of a receipt given to those who had bought *bulas de difuntos*. Immediate relief would come to the deceased suffering in purgatory when his name was placed in the appropriate blank:

> Y que consigan indulgencia y plenaria remission de todos sus pecados, por manera de ayuda y sufragio, porque libres de las penas de Purgatorio vayan sin impedimento alguno donde tendrán muy especial cuydado de rogar por quien tanto bien y limosna les hizo. Y por quanto vos _____ distes los dichos dos reales por el anima de _____ y recebistes en vos esta Bula, es ortogada al anima por quien distes essa cantidad las gracias y indulgencia plenaria sobredichas.[26]

Regardless of the amount of treasure laid up in heaven—there were questions as to whether or not it was infinite—alms-givers continued to draw on it. Needless to say, the practice was not discouraged by the pardoners, the *mercaderes*, or the government. But what is crucially important to my argument is the steadily increasing value that was placed on the bull as a document. Receipts of purchase or actual printed copies of the *bulas* may have been, from a skeptical (Protestant) viewpoint, worthless pieces of paper, at least spiritually. However, their massive consumption within Spain shows that they were clearly *thought* to possess miraculous power and authority. They were sacred texts whose spiritual value for the people was transformed into food for the revenue-starved government. Their economic worth was emphasized time and again, most notably by Philip II in his disputes with Pius V in the late 1560s.[27] They became a form of papal currency that the royal treasury exchanged for hard coinage. Innocent communities were duped into paying another form of taxation. On another level, as sacred *écriture* representing the institutional language of the Church, the *bulas de la cruzada* made their most successful crusades through the

---

O. F. M., autor de un *Tratado muy provechoso para todo fiel cristiano que quisiese saber el efecto de las indulgencias y perdones* [Seville, 1548], de que aunque algunos sumarios pusieran millares de años e indulgencias plenarias, no era cosa auténtica ni digna de ser creída, negando, además, rotundamente que en virtud de las bulas de Cruzada se saque ánima del purgatorio, y a que ni en Roma sabe nadie nada de tal privilegio ni consta en el texto de la bula" (Goñi Gaztambide, *Historia*, p. 511).

[25]Lea, "Indulgences," p. 129n.
[26]Quoted in *ibid.*, p. 130, n. 2.
[27]Lea, *History*, pp. 424–29; Goñi Gaztambide, "Los cuestores," pp. 39–43, 285–88.

manipulative rhetoric of the pardoners. Even the most suspecting congregations were vulnerable to their betraying speech and clever tricks.

There were of course many purchasers who believed in the spiritual efficacy of bulls and willingly bought them as soon as the pardoners came to town. The inhabitants of Sagra de Toledo were not of this type. Lázaro points out that his master "había predicado dos o tres días, haciendo sus acostumbradas diligencias, y no le habían tomado bula, ni a mi ver tenían intención de se la tomar. Estaba dado al diablo con aquello. . ." (p. 160). It is precisely this adversary relationship—which the *buldero* exploits—that leads to his success at the end of the chapter. He must not only persuade his skeptical audience to believe his words (sermon) but also move them to give alms for his wares (bulls). But in order to accomplish this double task, he first must win the sympathy of the community.

The pardoner's speech and actions are patterned after the *partes artes* of a forensic oration, as outlined by Quintilian: (1) *exordium*, (2) *narratio*, (3) *probatio*, (4) *refutatio*, and (5) *peroratio*.[28] The first of two rhetorical discourses that can be seen operating in the fifth *tratado* is introduced immediately following Lázaro's negative characterization of his master as compared with other pardoners he has met. The *buldero*'s self-presentation to the religious authorities is literally the *exordio* of the fiction with which he will seduce the congregation. He needs their sympathy and support because they have the power to produce his audience in the first place. Without their unwitting complicity there will be no victims.

> En entrando en los lugares do habían de presentar la bula, primero presentaba a los clérigos o curas algunas cosillas, no tampoco de mucho valor ni substancia: una lechuga murciana, si era por el tiempo; un par de limas o naranjas; un melocotón; un par de duraznos; cada sendas peras verdiniales. Ansí procuraba tenerlos propicios, porque favoresciesen su negocio y llamasen sus feligreses a tomar la bula (p. 158).

For a few bribes as worthless as the bulls he will preach the pardoner usurps the institutional authority of the Church. His *captatio benevolentiae* ("tenerlos propicios"), while directed toward the priests themselves, is focused much more on the appropriation of the power

---

[28]Lausberg, *Manual*, 1: 237–38; Quintilian, *Institutio oratoria*, 1: 514: "Nunc de iudiciali genere, quod est praecipue multiplex, sed officiis constat duobus intentionis ac depulsionis. Cuius partes, ut plurimus auctoribus placuit, quinque sunt: prooemium, narratio, probatio, refutatio, peroratio."

they represent, a force that can gather his audience into one place and provides the space where he will work out his trickery.

His having won over the religious authorities, however, does not imply a similarly easy victory over their "feligreses." Nor does his ability to speak their "language"—both literally and figuratively—bestow on his own "gentil y bien cortado romance" (p. 159) any special privilege. The pardoner's speech is already superior to theirs, for by probing them through language he is able to ascertain whether they "eran de reverendos" (circumspect) or "con reverendas se ordenan" (corrupt) without betraying his own fraudulent nature. The *buldero*, then, is engaged in a contractual exchange that is based on a double bribery, of things and words. In the end the sacred words of his *bulas* are exchanged for money. And the method he uses to effect such an exchange is the subject of the one experience that Lázaro presents to Vuestra Merced: " . . . diré uno muy sotil y donoso, con el cual probaré bien su suficiencia" (*ibid.*).

After establishing the framework and context in which his experience is to be understood, Lázaro begins the pardoner's *narratio* (a *narratio credibilis*), which at first glance seems to undermine the preceeding *exordium* by alienating his prospective victims altogether. The *buldero* and the *alguacil* meet "a jugar la colación" (p. 160), and during their meeting they end up insulting one another. The pardoner calls the constable a thief, and the constable responds in kind by labeling his companion a liar. Each goes for a weapon, but the potentially violent encounter is broken up by the "huéspedes y vecinos," who are drawn by the noise. And as if the constable's accusations might be unclear or ignored, Lázaro repeats them twice: " . . . el alguacil dijo a mi amo que era falsario y las bulas que predicaba que eran falsas" (*ibid.*); " . . . el pueblo se juntó, el cual andaba murmurando de las bulas, diciendo cómo eran falsas y que el mesmo alguacil, riñendo, lo había descubierto" (p. 161). The purpose of this scene, which takes place before the townsfolk,—although unclear to Lazarillo (and to ourselves) at the time,—is to establish the *argumentatio* (*probatio, refutatio*) at a high emotional level. The public can not be allowed to remain indifferent. The pardoner in this case pushes an already suspicious audience to the point of an active hatred toward his mission: " . . . tras que tenían mala gana de tomalla, con aquello [the constable's remarks] del todo la aborrescieron" (*ibid.*). The people, in their role as judges, are firmly on the side of the *alguacil* and thus identify themselves with what they believe to be the truth of civil authority. They have played into the pardoner's hands, as it were, for it

[69]

is easier to persuade an already hostile jury to one's favor than to win its sympathy if it is only partially involved in the debate on the issue at hand (*quaestio finito*). The orator has only to refute the credibility of his opponent (*refutatio*) to transfer a favorable response to himself (*confirmatio*). Or to put it more explicitly, the use of *indignatio* (part of the process of *confirmatio*) leads the public to reject the speaker's adversary: " . . . indignatio est oratio per quam conficitur, ut in aliquem hominem magnum odium aut in rem gravis offensio concitetur."[29] By replacing the constable's words with his own the pardoner not only confirms his sympathetic position but also assumes the constable's power—his credibility—through his appeal to a higher authority (God). He literally appropriates the constable's language.

We can summarize the pardoner's strategy up to this point in the following way: He must establish the constable's words as irrefutable truth in the eyes of the *feligreses*. The constable must be seen to defend the rights of the people. His role is to root out corruption, to protect the citizenry from swindlers like the pardoner. A closer look at the transfer of linguistic power will reveal the structural configuration of the process of transfer. The pardoner is involved in a double persuasion. His strategy demands that he first establish the efficacy and believability of his speech and then use the power he has gained on behalf of his speech to persuade the congregation of the validity of his *bulas*. There are, then, two parts to his overall strategy, the second depending directly on the first: If he is able to capture good will toward his words (*captatio benevolentiae*), he will automatically convince his listeners of the miraculous nature of the printed texts he offers for sale. They will be moved to act (*movere*) and will buy his false documents. But the fact that the pardoner succeeds in his project is not as important as the way he structures the plot that leads to his success. His perfectly symmetrical fiction (*argumentatio*) governs the responses of his audience and, consequently, the outcome of the deception:

| I | | II | |
|---|---|---|---|
| *A* | "Buenos hombres" (constable) | $A_1$ | "Buenos hombres" (pardoner) |
| *B* | Pardoner's prayer (speech) | $B_1$ | Pardoner's *bulas* (text) |
| *C* | Constable's seizure (efficacy of speech) | $C_1$ | Constable's exorcism (efficacy of text) |

[29]Cicero, *De Inventione*, in *De Optimo genere oratorum, Topica*, ed. and trans. H. M. Hubbell, Loeb Classical Library (London, 1949), p. 150; Lausberg, *Manual*, 1: 365:

| D Persuasion of congre-<br>gation (*captatio bene-*<br>*volentiae*) | ⟶ | $D_1$ Persuasion of congre-<br>gation (*movere*) |

The above diagram is nothing more than a static rendition of the movement from the first column to the second: The constable's speech to the audience ("Buenos hombres, oídme una palabra. . ." [*ibid.*] is followed by the pardoner's prayer ("—Señor Dios, a quien ninguna cosa es escondida. . ." [p. 162]), whose effect is to deprive the constable of his power to speak (". . . comenzó a bramar y echar espumajos por la boca y torcella. . ." [p. 163]). Having refuted his opponent, the pardoner wins the good will of the people by transforming the constable's words of truth into lies: "—Bien se le emplea, pues levantaba tan falso testimonio—" (*ibid.*). He now addresses his listeners (column II) using the same introductory words the constable used before: "—Buenos hombres, vosotros nunca habíades de rogar por un hombre en quien Dios tan señaladamente se ha señalado. . ." (p. 164). The pardoner then delivers an extended "oración" (*ibid.*) and restores the constable's speech, not with his own words, but with the words of the bull: "Y esto hecho, mandó traer la bula y púsola en la cabeza. Y luego el pecador del alguacil comenzó, poco a poco, a estar mejor y tornar en sí" (p. 165). And as final proof of the *bula's* miraculous power, the constable testifies on behalf of its efficacy by asking forgiveness:

> Y desque fue bien vuelto en su acuerdo, echóse a los pies del señor comisario y demandóle perdón; y confesó haber dicho aquello por la boca y mandamiento del demonio, lo uno, por hacer a él daño y vengarse del enojo; lo otro, y más principal, porque el demonio reciba mucha pena del bien que allí se hiciera en tomar la bula" (*ibid.*).

The penitent attitude of the pardoner's formerly implacable enemy and the bull's ability to restore speech and sanity are more than enough to move the congregation: "Y a tomar la bula hubo tanta priesa, que casi ánima viviente en el lugar no quedó sin ella, marido y mujer, y hijos y hijas, mozos y mozas" (*ibid.*). The pardoner's sacred text now speaks for itself, not because it is a papal document, but because he has merged its linguistic power with his own. He has succeeded in turning it into a physical object—a relic—to be possessed. It in turn "possesses" its purchasers by the very nature of the linguistic contract the *buldero* has created. The fiction of the text, then, produces those consumers

---

". . . es como un trallazo sobre el público para que se indisponga con la causa de la parte contraria."

[71]

who enter into its illusion; and their entry is made possible by their acceptance of the notion that language actually can construct and deconstruct reality. That texts such as papal bulls exist at all is ample proof of the fact that at the basis of written language is a myth of salvation: Souls can be taken from purgatory and even from hell; crimes of the living can be forgiven and their punishment remitted; and in our specific case, a mad man can be brought to sanity.

While writing silences an author's speaking voice, the text it produces guarantees his permanent "existence" beyond his own voice, as well as the voices of others. Lázaro's transformation from town crier to author, from speaker to writer, is an act of self-salvation from the destructive gossip of his neighbors. The story of the *buldero* is included in his *Vida*, not so much to satirize such sixteenth-century abuses as to disclose how such deceptions are performed.[30] Laying bare the *argumentatio* of the pardoner is simultaneously a revelation of Lázaro's strategy, which lies behind the presentation of his own text to Vuestra Merced. One fundamental difference makes Lázaro's project far more significant and vital. The pardoner stands in a slightly contiguous relationship to his text, whereas Lázaro *is* his text. The pardoner is preaching the institutional documents of the Church. He did not write them; rather he brings them alive, as it were, with his rhetoric. Lázaro, on the other hand, is presenting the *entera noticia* of himself. He produces the text and is produced by it. The pardoner may lose money; Lázaro may lose altogether his hard-won experience and position if he is not successful in "selling" his text. In essence, his life is at stake.

Both Lázaro and the pardoner face skeptical audiences. Lázaro admits that the rumors circulating in Toledo are true; he claims simultaneously, however, that he is no worse than his gossiping neighbors. The people of Sagra de Toledo have heard and witnessed that the pardoner and the constable conspired to defraud them. They were present when the constable accused the pardoner of being a "falsario" (p. 160) and said that the "bulas que predicaba que eran falsas" (*ibid.*). The constable's "Buenos hombres" speech not only repeats his previous accusation but also discloses their conspiracy: "Yo vine aquí con este echacuervo que os predica, el cual me engañó, y dijo que le favoresciese en este negocio, y que partiríamos la ganancia" (p. 161). The truth of both *casos*, then, is made available to their respective audiences. And finally, both narrators seek to make themselves less evil

[30]Cf. Durand, "The Author and Lázaro," p. 99: "The core of the episode is one of social criticism; the form, an elaborately developed 'joke' on townspeople."

and grasping than they are. The pardoner presents himself as being victimized by the constable's words; Lázaro makes himself an undeserving victim of the gossip and of the archpriest (see chapter VII). The outcomes of their *casos* are also related. The pardoner persuades his audience to receive the document that he preaches. Lázaro must persuade his reader of the efficacy of his text through the language with which he writes it.

The pardoner, then, energizes the already sacred language of the Church with his rhetorical artistry, whereas Lázaro articulates his life through the "grosero estilo" of the *homo litteratus*. His is the language of honor and reputation, of one's standing in the community. He sustains honor as a social code on one level and redefines it on another: He is both *pregonero* and author of his life. His quest for honor is also based on a discourse of analogy: *Honra* is a word whose semantic value, he argues, is perceived through the linguistic community that defines it. He inherits the "new" honor of a writer whose peculiar literary birth is the conversion of the unwritten *logos* of himself as *pregonero* into written autobiography. Lázaro attempts to convert Vuestra Merced into another member of that "inocente gente" of Sagra de Toledo, who are so obsessed with appearance—with the *verbum visibile* through which they perceive themselves in the world—that they ae blinded to the nature of the "text" put before them. His revelation of the *buldero's* technique is a veiled dramatization of his own strategy to acquire the support of Vuestra Merced. Implicit in it, however, is a threat of social excommunication: Vuestra Merced's association with Lázaro and the archpriest puts his own honorable position in jeopardy. Ultimately, Lázaro's life story is another kind of *bula*, one that is made to speak for itself. The power of its rhetoric will determine the mode of its author's salvation and "buen puerto."

## VI

Buldas [Bulas] hay en Roma y espadas en Cuéllar
*Anonymous**

Por ventura, en el vestir, ¿vístese como quiere? No por
cierto, sino como a los otros ve.

*Antonio de Guevara*

Lazarillo calls himself an "hombre de bien" in the sixth *tratado* as
a result of the "hábito" that he is able to buy (p. 171). First he
becomes an *hombre de negocios*, for it is through his contractual
relationship with the *capellán* that he earns the money with which he
buys the "ropa vieja" and which allows him to advance beyond the
menial *oficio* of a water seller. He ends up investing his earnings,
however, in the same *verbum visibile* of honor ("ahorré para me vestir
honradamente") that characterized the *escudero*, and thus falls victim to
the same system of values. There is one fundamental difference
between their respective techniques for acquiring an honorable
situation: In Toledo's economic system the squire had nothing to
exchange, nothing to give value to his empty words and costume.
Lazarillo perceived the squire's weakness—his lack of money—and
attempts to protect himself from an ignominious failure like the
squire's by entering into a financially productive relationship with the
*capellán*: "Daba cada día a mi amo treinta maravedís ganados, y los
sábados ganaba para mí, todo lo demás, entre semana, de treinta
maravedís" (*ibid.*). Working for someone else for more than basic
sustenance, however, is unsatisfactory because it precludes the
honorable life he seeks. He cannot be simultaneously an "hombre de
bien" and an *aguador*: "Desque me vi en hábito de hombre de bien, dije
a mi amo se tomase su asno, que no quería más seguir aquel oficio"
(*ibid.*). He will seek instead a more powerful association, not one that
limits him exclusively to a master-servant relationship, but one that
connects him with an institutional hierarchy that extends even to the

*Francisco Rodríguez Marín includes this proverb in *12.600 refranes más*, p. 45a. He
also includes an explanatory note: "Parece ser una frase, conservada tradicionalmente
que se atribuyera a don Pedro I de Castilla cuando, para casar con doña Juana de Castro,
obligó a los obispos de Ávila y Salamanca a que dijeran a la doña Juana que él era libre del
casamiento con doña Blanca, a lo cual ellos se prestaron 'con muy grand miedo que
ovieron.' "

king. In the final *tratado* he obtains an *oficio real* as the *pregonero* of Toledo.

Lazarillo's introduction to the world of *negocios* is a gradual process that begins with the *escudero*'s notable lack of success, takes form through the *fraile*'s hidden but effective sexual trafficking, and establishes itself definitively for Lazarillo through the *buldero*'s mastery of oral language. While he is serving the squire, for example, the word *negocio(s)* is associated with the business community of Toledo and with Lazarillo. The squire complains about the "señores . . . [who] no quieren ver en sus casas hombres virtuosos; antes los aborrescen y tienen en poco y llaman nescios, y que no son personas de negocios ni con quien el señor se puede descuidar" (p. 152). And later when the *escribano* and the *alguacil* begin to take inventory of the squire's belongings, they speak of their lucrative find ("que está bueno el negocio" [p. 154]), ultimately complaining, however, of the "otro negocio que les importaba más por venir a aquél" (p. 155). Lazarillo himself is bitter that the squire has left him with his "negocios tan al revés" (*ibid.*). The *escudero*, as we have already remarked, can exchange words only; his weakness stems from his inability to convert words into money. The friar's "negocios seglares," on the other hand, are defined in terms of his "trote," his manipulation of women as sexual goods. The *buldero*'s trade, as Lazarillo observes, depends on the fruit and vegetables that he gives the local clergy to "tenerlos propicios, porque favoresciesen su negocio" (p. 158) and on his "bien cortado romance y desenvoltísima lengua" (p. 159), with which he seduces the congregation. In terms of the ideas of language that I have been attempting to elaborate, it is possible to detect a slight movement from language as visibility (the *verbum visibile* of honor), as silence ("otras cosillas que no digo"), and as forensic oratory—rhetoric and the art of persuasion ("comienza una oración no menos larga que devota, con la cual hizo llorar a toda la gente" [p. 164]; "Y a tomar la bula hubo tanta priesa, que casi ánima viviente en el lugar no quedó sin ella [the *bula*]" [p. 165]). Each of these economies can be reduced to verbal formulations that help to place Lazarillo's success as a water seller in its proper context:

1. *escudero* / *trocar* ("que saldría a la plaza a trocar una pieza de a dos" [p. 153]);

2. *fraile* / *trotar* ("ni yo pude con su trote durar más" [p. 157]); and

3. *buldero* / *industriar* ("conoscí como había sido industriado por el industrioso y inventivo de mi amo" [p. 165]).

[75]

Most important for our argument is the fact that the pardoner's success is based directly on his speech and cunning, a lesson that Lazarillo does not forget, for it is his mouth—his voice—that effects his own prosperity: "Este fue el primer escalón que yo subí para venir a alcanzar buena vida, *porque mi boca era medida*" (pp. 170–71), emphasis mine). Lazarillo's good life, then, depends on his voice—that is, on the ability of his voice to sell his products. In other words, the mouth is the measure of the man. In the first *tratado* it held the coins he kept from the *ciego*; here it is the source of the *maravedís* that he uses to purchase his honorable "hábito de hombre de bien"; and in the final *tratado* it defines his existence as the voice of Toledo. He learned from the squire that words are not money, that they cannot be exchanged ("trocar") within a system that is based on hard cash. The friar's "negocios seglares" and his apparent success depend on his ability to offer a service ("trote") that is perpetually in demand. The pardoner, Lazarillo notes, sells neither himself nor a service, but rather an object that can be possessed for a sum of money. His success involves a much more complicated enterprise, one built on conspiracy, rhetorical mastery, and trickery ("industrioso y inventivo"). Lazarillo's economy is like that of the pardoner in that it is based on the persuasive power of his voice to sell water. Lazarillo's value system, however, is an extension of the squire's since the money he saves is invested in the outer signs of honor and status. This curious marriage of language and economy, creates for Lazarillo a space within which secular honor and the institutional power of speech work together to produce the "buena vida" he seeks. From now on, he will depend exclusively on his mastery over oral language to bring him both money and position within Toledo's society. In sum, then, Lazarillo's economy is linguistic in nature, for at its base the two verbs that characterize it best, *ganar* and *comprar*, are causally related to his voice:

> Fueme tan bien en el oficio, que al cabo de cuatro años que lo usé, con poner en la ganancia buen recaudo, ahorré para me vestir muy honradamente de la ropa vieja. De la cual compré un jubón de fustán . . . (p. 171).

Earning ("ganancia"), collecting his share ("recaudo") saving ("ahorré"), and buying ("compré") reflect a detailed economic process whose final phase reveals his total investment in another system—honor—in which working for one's living is prohibited. Thus he rejects his *oficio* as a water seller in favor of an identity that will not tolerate manual labor. In other words, he moves from *doing* to *being* as the foundation of his new life as an "hombre de bien."

Lazarillo's rejection of his contractual arrangement with the *capellán* after he attains what he believes to be an honorable profession—simply being a man of worth—constitutes another way of disclosing the total reorganization of the myth of money in his life. Now *money* will work for *him*. This rejection is also an echo of the first episode in the sixth *tratado*; thus it confirms his decision to base further investments in professions that are primarily or totally dependent on his talent as *homo loquens*. Whether his serving a "maestro de pintar panderos" (p. 170) is an allusion to his role in helping his master trick unsuspecting people out of their money, as Bataillon suggests,[1] or points to the theme of honor, because of the relationship that such employment would have with the nobility, as Blecua notes,[2] Lazarillo's explicit reference to the *nonverbal* nature of his duties ("para molelle los colores") contrasts sharply with the necessary verbal skill required by his next role, that of *aguador*. He mentions this *oficio* so that he can reveal his failure to attain the good life through manual labor ("también sufrí mil males"). Language, he seems to emphasize, forms an integral part of his *Vida* from the beginning, and any occupation not centrally concerned with it will be at best financially unsuccessful and at worst physically dangerous, as he points out when he abandons the *alguacil* in the seventh *tratado*.

[1]*Novedad*, pp. 65–66: ". . . la comparación de dos curiosos proverbios—*Según sea el dinero será el pandero* y *Quien tiene dineros pinta panderos*—permite imaginar una vieja historieta española, paralela a la del *Ulenspiegel*, en la cual un falso pintor de panderos habría engañado a una humilde clientela pueblerina, haciéndose, él también, pagar por adelantado."

[2]Blecua, p. 170, reminds us that "la voz *pintapanderos* tenía significado despectivo . . ." (cf. Mateo Alemán, *Ortografía castellano* [1609], ed. J.R. Garcidueñas [México City, 1950], pp. 8–9. Blecua also notes—basing his argument on the context of *pandero* in the *Pícara Justina*—that "el *pandero*, o bien o no es un instrumento musical, o éste y su pintura tenían íntima relación con la nobleza de una familia. Sería, por tanto, una anticipación del tema de la honra de tanta importancia en este *tratado*" (p. 171). Lázaro's mention of his association with a "pinta panderos" may allude to activities less honorable than those suggested by Blecua. Gonzalo Fernández de Oviedo, *Las quinquagenas de la nobleza de España* ca. 1546–56), ed. Vicente de la Fuente (Madrid, 1880), p. 339, adds another proverb concerning the figure of the *pandero*: "No tiene juyzio sano / El que cree de ligero: / Ni lo que dize el pandero / Suele ser todo verdad." The implications of these verses coincide with Bataillon's interpretation of the *pandero* as a deceiver, a liar. Fortunately Fernández de Oviedo gives us his own interpretation; for him *pandero* is a metaphor: " . . . e asi essa metaphora del pandero no quiso aqui sinificar que los ombres no se deuen escuchar todas vezes. Y por la manera de la musica, tan baxa e vil, se está entendido lo que en ella se suele tratar, que son lagoterias y desuarios, e fabulas, e mentiras, resçitadas al son de las sonajas. Pues, si los panderos son adufles [*sic*] de mugeres, cantarán con ellos lo que ellas saben, que son cantiçios libidinosos de amores desuanitados, y de mal tono y peor proposito, que, ni discrepen de luxuria, ni traygan prouecho a casa ni al barrio, sino a fin de leuantar moças, y

Returning now to what seems to be the first achievement worth recording, namely, his becoming an *aguador*, we must determine in what sense it constitutes a success, how it relates to his experience with the *escudero*, and finally, what role it plays in the total life of which it is a part. For Lazarillo success is measured in terms of his ability to "alcanzar buena vida," which in turn is defined within this *tratado* as leading the life of an "hombre de bien." But leading such a life, as we have mentioned already, consists of dressing in a certain way; that is, the ontological status of a gentleman resides in the visible language spoken by his clothes. Success, then, is not financial security or self-sufficiency, but rather the ability to put on—literally—the signs of honor. His talent for making money is of secondary importance insofar as it leads to what Lazarillo views as a much more fundamentally crucial transformation of his life. To be rid of the identity of the *oficio* he must reject it; he must move to a higher social plane of an institutional nature. In other words, his private contract with the *capellán* is exchanged for a public social contract, the civil bond of a government position. If Lazarillo serves anyone, it will be the king, not a lowly, venal chaplain whose alleged vow of poverty and service to God is a camouflage for his mercantile activity, which originates within the Church itself ("entrando un dia en la iglesia mayor, un capellán della me recibió por suyo" [*ibid.*]).[3] Lazarillo severs his connection from an *oficio*, which by its nature offers no honorable status; at the same time, he rebels against his exploited condition, searching for an economic system that will value him for his identity rather than for his money-making abilities. It is this final decision that reveals his vulnerability—his blindness—to the *verbum vesibile* of honor: Lazarillo interprets it within the value system of the *escudero*, whereas it is meant to be interpreted as an integral part of the contemporary social marketplace of Toledo, or, to quote Guevara again, through the eyes of "los ostros." Moreover, Lazarillo's choice of the various pieces of clothing that constitute his new identity as a gentleman is a self-revealing act of another kind, for it provides us with the first indications of the

aperçebirlas a mal obrar, e de buenas hazerlas peores de lo que serian sin esa musica de cascaueles cubiertos."

[3]Molho argues that both the "pinta panderos" and the "capellán" function as signs of mercantile activity: "En fait, tout ce Sixième Traité (qui tient en une vingtaine de lignes) traite de marchandise: marchandise banale et légitime (celle de l'artisan) qui s'oppose, dans l'esprit de l'humaniste, à la marchandise indue dont fait son profit l'homme d'Eglise" (*Romans picaresques espagnols, p.xxv,n*). Albert Sicroff, "Sobre el estilo del *Lazarillo de Tormes*," *NRFH* 11 (1957). 157–70, and Emilio Carilla, "Cuatro notas sobre el *Lazarillo*," *RFE* 43 (1960): 97–116, state that the episode of the "pinta panderos" is completely irrelevant to the novel.

anonymous author's ridicule and eventual condemnation of his narrator.

Virtually every reader of the *Lazarillo* has referred to the correspondences between the third and sixth *tratados*: Lazarillo's desire to be an "hombre de bien" echoes the squire's remarks on the "caudal de los hombres de bien" (p. 148); his investment in a costume to acquire an honorable status mimicks the squire's association of honor and dress; his rejection of labor as a legitimate, honorable activity is surely comparable to the squire's refusal to work or to serve anyone beneath his dignity; and finally, both view speech as production, as the basis for assimilation into Toledo's society. The squire's efforts fail, of course, whereas Lazarillo's succeed at least in his own mind, because of his activities as an *hombre de negocios*. Of all these similarities, the one that is most prominent (and makes up half of the sixth *tratado*) is the association between clothing and honor. A detailed analysis of their respective costumes not only reveals the extent to which Lazarillo perceives the squire as a model to be imitated but also points to his blindness, his inability to understand fully the consequences of the identity he has created for himself. Like the squire, he has fallen victim to the notion that the language of honor is solely a system of visible signs.

When Lazarillo first meets the squire, he notices his "razonable vestido" (p. 130). Later we discover that its basic elements consist of "calzas, y jubón, y sayo y capa" (p. 136). No further details are provided, however, and we are left with a description that might apply to the clothes of any gentleman. The one item of the squire's dress that merits more description is his sword:

> —¡Oh, si supieres, mozo, que pieza es ésta! No hay marco de oro en el mundo por que yo la diese; mas ansí, ninguna de cuantas Antonio hizo, no certó a ponelle los aceros tan prestos como ésta los tiene (*ibid.*).

He gives it a double value and in doing so doubly inflates his self-esteem. The sword owns the squire. The first value is monetary, created by his words, not by the actual cash he would receive were he to sell it. It is a symbol of the money he lacks, of his poverty and hypocrisy. The second value—the sword's inherent quality—is also established by the squire's words. It is sharper, hence better, than any of those made by the legendary Antonio. The squire's use of the double negative ("ninguna . . . no") emphasizes both the sword's worthlessness and the fact that Antonio did not create it. Through double-talk he succeeds in convincing Lazarillo of the sword's worth, not because of its sharpness but through its linguistically redefined social function. Its real value is as an object to be seen or, as it is here, as an excuse for conversation. The squire, then, overvalues his sword in the same way that he overrates himself: His economy of honor is circular in nature, for it begins and ends at the level of language.

Turning now to Lazarillo's description of the clothes and sword he buys, we detect an immediate difference in the concreteness of its detail:

| *Escudero* | Lazarillo |
|---|---|
| "jubón" | "jubón de fustán viejo" |
| "sayo" | "sayo raído de manga tranzada y puerta" |
| "capa" | "capa que había sido frisada" |
| "espada" | "una espada de las viejas primeras de Cuéllar" |
| "calzas" | [       ] |

The *escudero*'s clothing must have been of sufficient style and quality to persuade his landlord to rent him a house on credit; his poverty is not revealed by discrepancies between the position he seeks to maintain and the clothes he wears. Lazarillo, however, commits a serious blunder when he buys a replica of the squire's costume and draws our attention to it when he describes each piece in detail.[4] His clothing, and more importantly, his description of it, would not have gone unnoticed by his neighbors in Toledo or by sixteenth-century readers of his *Vida*. It seems, according to Carmen Bernis Madrazo,[5] that Lazarillo purchased only high-quality merchandise. For instance, the *jubón* made of *fustán*, a material usually imported from Italy, was of

[4]Truman, "Parody and Irony," states that "Lázaro presents himself in his new attire and eminence in such a way as to indicate that it enters into his attention to laugh at himself playing the part he now chose to play" (p. 604); C. B. Morris, "Lázaro and the Squire: 'Hombres de bien,' " *BHS* 41 (1964): 238–41, on the other hand, concludes that Lázaro's clothing makes him "feel a different man; to be seen now with the ass (which has served him well) is as great an indignity for him as it is for the squire to be connected with his servant" (p. 240). Irony in the *Lazarillo*,—which is treated very shrewdly by Truman— seems to extend beyond Lázaro and Vuestra Merced; if anyone is laughing, it is the anonymous author, who laughs at both his characters and his readers.

[5]*Indumentaria española en tiempos de Carlos V* (Madrid, 1962). See also María José Saez Piñuela, *La moda en la corte de Felipe II* (Madrid, 1962); and Abelardo Carrillo y Gariel, *El traje en la nueva España* (Mexico City, 1959). I have not had access to contemporary texts, such as that of Juan de Acelga, *Libro de geometría . . . y traça el cual trata de lo tocante al officio de sastre* (Madrid, 1580), which might give us more detail about clothing and the various materials with which it was made in the sixteenth century.

exceptional quality. The *Ordenanzas de sastres, jubeteros, ropavexeros y calceteros de Granada* (1541) pointed out that while the usual filler used in *jubones* was "algodón y angeo," those that were made of *fustán* were to be filled with "lana fina y lavada," [6] which testifies to the fact that garments made of fustian were given special treatment. Not only does the use of fustian point to a *jubón* of finer, softer cloth; it also implies that wearers of such high quality clothing are themselves of equally high worth and prestige. But the obviously significant addition of the word *viejo* undermines the honorable appearance that Lazarillo has attempted to create. Unable to buy new clothes with the few *maravedís* he has saved, he broadcasts his poverty by acquiring an old and used *jubón*.

This same process of unwitting self-disclosure is also at work in his description of the *sayo*, the *capa*, and the *espada*. The *sayo* too is second hand ("raído"). The words that refer to its style are more important, however, than those that refer to the quality of the material. His sleeves are literally braided, that is, they are gathered sleeves (a possible version of the so-called "mangas borrachas"?),[7] as opposed to the loose, open *musequíes*, which were characteristic, according to Torquemada, of an earlier style.[8] The same can be said of the *puerta* mentioned by Lazarillo, even though it is also included by Torquemada in his description of outmoded clothing.[9] In the sixteenth century the *puerta* was "una pieza cuadrada con que se cerraba el delantero de los sayos, . . . pero se daba también, sin duda, a otros tipos de cerramiento de los vestidos." [10] While it was still a part of the *sayo* circa 1530, a sculpture of a *caballero* of the time reveals that it was not used (at least in this case) to close the tunic. Bernis Madrazo describes the sculpture as a "caballero con la puerta del sayo desatada." [11] It is of course impossible to determine the function—practical or cosmetic—it plays in Lazarillo's

[6]Bernis Madrazo, *Indumentaria*, p. 94.

[7]I have followed Blecua's reading, i.e., that "tranzada" should be read as *trenzada*. However, another interpretation can be based on the word *tranzada*, which means "cortada," or "destruida" (Joan Corominas, *Diccionario crítico etimológico de la lengua castellana*, 4 vols. [Bern, 1954], 4:543−44). Corominas cites Leguina's *Glosario de voces de armería*, p. 857: " . . . piezas del arnés cortados horizontalmente en varios trozos, unidos por enganches de resbalón." "Tranzada," then, could refer to shortened or cut sleeves or even to the sleeves that are "destruidas" from having been previously owned. Hence "manga tranzada" would balance "sayo raído."

[8]Antonio de Torquemada, *Coloquios satíricos*, ed. M. Menéndez Pelayo, Nueva Biblioteca de Autores Españoles, vol. 7 (Madrid, 1907), pp. 485−581; the quotation comes from p. 528b.

[9]*Ibid*.: " . . . traínlos escotados como camisas de mujeres, y una puerta muy pequeña."

[10]Bernis Madrazo, *Indumentaria*, p. 100.

[11]*Ibid*.

costume—but the fact that it is referred to at all may point to the outmoded nature of his *sayo*. *Sayos* with *puertas* are referred to frequently in documents of the first thirty years of the century. Iconographical evidence suggests that soon afterward the *sayo* was worn closed, which would seem to eliminate the necessity of a *puerto*.[12] Certainly the *puerta* had lost its indumentarian sense by the time that Covarrubias compiled his dictionary, for he fails to record any reference to its relationship with clothing.

Establishing any firm connection between a chronological development of style and Lazarillo's clothing is virtually impossible, given the fact that such a *système de la mode* was constantly changing.[13] One of Torquemada's interlocutors claimed to be an eye-witness to these changes: " . . .lo que peor es, que cuando un hombre piensa que está vestido para diez años, no es pasado uno cuando viene otro uso nuevo que luego le pone en cuidado."[14] What is emphasized in Lazarillo's inventory is, not the style, but the fact that everything he buys was owned by someone before him. A *capa*, for instance, that "había sido frisada" (p. 171) did not lose its nap because of its age but because it had been worn off, so consumed that it could not be reconstituted. The same can be said of the *sayo* and, by implication, of the final item listed, the *espada*. While the other articles of clothing together would form a conservative outfit, the addition of the sword, with its particular historical provenance, turns the entire ensemble into an absurdly anachronistic costume.

It is not a coincidence that Lazarillo's sword comes from Cuéllar—a city famous for its swordmakers and perhaps more importantly from our viewpoint, for the fact that it was the city where Antonio maintained a forge.[15] We recall that neither Lazarillo nor the squire claims to own a sword made in fact by the famous *espadero*. Rather they lay claim to his reputation by association, the squire mentioning his

[12]See *ibid.*, pl. 93: "Caballero con la puerta del sayo desatada."

[13]Cf. Rico, ed., *Lazarillo*, p. 76n.: " . . . es difícil concluir algo sobre la fecha del *Lazarillo* en la base de este pasaje, . . . "

[14]*Coloquios satíricos*, p. 529; cf. Guevara, *Aviso de privados*, p. 54: "En la religión vístense a menos costa de hacienda y a más consolación de la persona, que no en la corte; porque el pobre cortesano y caballero, más mudas ha de hacer de ropas que no los halcones de plumas."

[15]Cf. Rico, *La novela picaresca española*, p. 76n; Blecua, p. 171n. Although Balbino Velasco Bayon's book, *Historia de Cuéllar* (Segovia, 1974), which runs to more than 530 pages, contains a section on the history of industry, there is no space to include any discussion of Cuéllar's famous swordmakers. Miguel Capella Martínez, *La industria en Madrid*, 2 vols. (Madrid, 1962), 1: 336, states that the squire's reference to Antonio is to Antonio Ruiz of Madrid-Toledo, "espadero del rey."

name and Lazarillo his place of residence. Moreover, they differ in the way the association is made. The squire refers to the sharpness of his sword, while Lazarillo refers to his as "una espada de las viejas primeras de Cuéllar." Lazarillo attaches himself to its lineage, its birthplace, as it were, to the very origins of swordmaking in Cuéllar: Not only is the sword old, it is one of the first swords made there. He may in fact not be referring to Antonio (since he does not mention him) but rather to the honor and nobility associated with swords from Cuéllar, that is, to those who made them valuable through ownership. And that is precisely the kind of value Lazarillo seeks; he is concerned, not with their practical value as well-made weapons, but with their valuable appearance as *espadas roperas*, as swords to be worn in public as signs of worth, of an "hombre de bien."

In February of 1560 Beltrán de la Cueva, the third duke of Alburquerque, died in Toledo. He was not only "uno de los más valerosos y esforzados caballeros que en tiempo del emperador Carlos V hubo en España" [16] but also "señor de Cuéllar," overseeing the first *Ordenanzas de la villa* in 1546.[17] Contained in the *Inventario* of his possessions is a list of "espadas roperas," in which we find the following descriptions:

> Una espada ancha, de las de Antonius, con su guarnición dorada y contera de plata alemana, e vaina de terciopelo carmesí. . . . Otra espada de canal, vieja, ancha e con unas letras en que dicen *Juanes me fezió*. E en medio della una *P* dentro de una onda partida, con su guarnición portoguesa, barnizada, fluecos e puño de sirgo negro, e correas dobladas de cuero negro, con cabos e hebillas barnizadas, e vaina de cuero negro. Hízola Juan de Lobingez, en Cuéllar.[18]

The point of my digression is not to suggest or even to hint at a connection between the duke of Alburquerque and the ignoble Lazarillo de Tormes, rather it is to draw attention to a sixteenth-century commentary in the same document on a sword made by Antonio (not identified as being from Cuéllar) and one made by the Cuéllar artisan Juan de Lobíngez. The Lobíngez weapon produced a much more detailed description despite the fact that the Antonio sword seems to be a richer object, its colors ("guarnición dorada,"

[16]Velasco Bayon, *Historia de Cuéllar*, p. 286.
[17]*Ibid.*, p. 287.
[18]Enrique de Leguina, *La espada: Apuntes para su historia en España* (Seville, 1885), p. 28n; I have not been able to see the entire inventory (which lists clothing as well), published by Antonio Rodríguez Villa in *RABM* 9 (1883): 17–37, 66–80, 99–104: "Inventario del moviliario, alhajas, ropas, armería y otros efectos. . . . "

"plata alemana," "terciopelo carmesí") standing in stark contrast to blackness ("sirgo negro," "cuero negro," "vaina de cuero negro"). What is stressed in the description of the Cuéllar sword is its antiquity, oddly enough, the same characteristic emphasized by Lazarillo. What seems to be most significant, however, is that both swords were owned by a nobleman from Cuéllar: His noble genealogy is linked to the genealogy of his weapons. Cuéllar swords, or swords associated with Cuéllar, bespeak nobility and honor and strongly point to Lazarillo's motivation in associating himself, with the same value system, as a slavish imitator of the squire and as an "hombre de bien." He seeks to be identified through the visible sign of *la negra honra* and prestige; he is unable to detect, however, that the sword does not make the man, that it is the inherent quality of the man that bestows value on the weapon.

Lazarillo's reference to his sword all but completes the indumentary model built on the squire. Only one item remains: the "calzas," which will serve both as the conclusion to our reading of the sixth *tratado* and as the introduction to the seventh and final installment of Lazarillo's *Vida*.

The absence of the stockings in our model may be puzzling at first glance, especially in light of the fact that Lazarillo seems to have tried so diligently to be a complete remake of his former master. However, as Bernis Madrazo has pointed out, " . . . de las dos prendas que en el siglo XVI se usaban para cubrir las piernas y el cuerpo hasta la cintura, las calzas eran la propia de los hombres que vestían a la moda." [19] It is difficult to believe that Lázaro forgot to mention them or failed to include them because they were unnecessary parts of his total costume. The clothes he buys so exactly repeat the squire's "razonable vestido" that he surely would not omit one of the most stylish components.

The silence surrounding the stockings here is the same silence associated with footwear elsewhere in the novel. The used stockings that would match the used clothing he has been able to buy are provided only in the seventh *tratado*, by the archpriest. They function as signs of Lazarillo's final dishonor. The honor, then, that is implied in the ownership of a Cuéllar sword is swept away by the dishonor so clearly symbolized by the wearing of another man's stockings. The "primer escalón" he has climbed to "alcanzar buena vida" belongs on a low ladder indeed; he ascends from the level of an "hombre de bien" to that of an agreeable cuckold.

[19]*Indumentaria*, p. 79.

Lázaro's adventures as a cuckold, as we will see, are materially pleasant as long as he is able to control the voices of those around him, that is, as long as he uses his own voice to silence those of his neighbors. The authority behind speech, then, is the area where the ultimate power of censorship—both social and linguistic—resides, and for Lázaro this power in the sixth *tratado* is his status as an "hombre de bien," a position he clearly sees as being superior to that of a *capellán*. The grammatical structure of the final sentence *is* the social structure that exists between himself and his master: " . . . dije a mi amo se tomase su asno . . . "(*ibid.*). He subordinates (subjoins) the *capellán*, turning him into a "dependent clause," the recipient of what Lázaro *tells* him to do. Imperatives function only when the power behind them is recognized by both speaker and hearer: Lázaro's voice, by producing money, is able to articulate a command understood by his venal master.

The economic foundation that lies behind the power of Lázaro's voice is firmly established by his financial and linguistic domination of the chaplain. While his voice now functions in a position of power, he fails to hear the other language he has chosen to speak: the *verbum visibile* of honor, the language spoken by his clothing. The yawning gap between what his clothes say and what he wants them to say is a space occupied by the author of the novel, who is no longer invisible behind his narrator. The author now points to the water seller who gives orders to a chaplain, to the ex-beggar who calls himself a man of worth. He dresses him in used clothing—purchased no doubt in some *almoneda*, a market that Lázaro himself knows well[20]—to call his attention to his poverty and pretense. He creates a buffoon who is unaware of his own buffoonery and provides him with the illusion of his self-determination in a society where everyone is subject to the desires of others. Lazarillo fails to see that he is not a squire, that dressing like his former master does not miraculously transform him into someone he is not. In sum, while Lazarillo's voice may be his own, his clothing belongs to others, or in the words of Guevara, "como a los otros ve."

[20] He tells us in the seventh *tratado:* "Y es que tengo cargo de pregonar los vinos que en esta ciudad se venden, *y en almonedas y cosas perdidas*" (p. 173, emphasis mine).

# VII

El pregonero no ha de ser mudo sino de clara e sonable e alta voz.

*Gonzalo Fernández de Oviedo*

Il suffit parfois d'une rumeur, d'un voisinage pour altérer l'honneur, même celui des modestes.

*Bartolomé Bennasssar*

The seventh and final *tratado* is a structural replication of the sixth: Lazarillo serves two masters in each, and in each his experience with the first master is nonverbal in nature (*moledor de colores / hombre de justicia*), whereas his experience with the second is a verbally defining role (*aguador / pregonero*). The shift in these professions reveals more than formally structured narrative or a repetition of symmetrical fortune reversals. He has literally become his voice, that is, his voice has produced both his good fortune and his identity:

|  | VI | VII |
|---|---|---|
| 1. | "sufrí mil males" *(moledor de colores)* | "oficio peligroso" *(hombre de justicia)* |
| 2. | "alcanzar buena vida" *(hombre de bien)* | "alcanzar lo que procuré" *(oficio real)* |

He has acquired visibility through the *verbum visibile* of honor, through the clothing he wears. He has talked himself into money, as it were, to give himself a social identity ("hombre de bien") within Toledo's economically based honor system. In this final *tratado* he succeeds in transforming this visible presence into substance: He obtains an *oficio real*.

Merely being an "hombre de bien," as he discovered through the squire, leads nowhere unless a compatible service relationship can be established in the larger community. At the end of the sixth *tratado*, for instance, Lazarillo gives up his source of income as *aguador* precisely because of the incompatible identity it produces. He searches for a respectable position with a guaranteed income for life, a position he

[86]

calls an *asiento,* and he finds it through the help of "amigos y señores" (p. 172)—as *pregonero* of Toledo:

> Y pensando en qué modo de vivir haría mi asiento, por tener descanso y ganar algo para la vejez, quiso Dios alumbrarme y ponerme en camino y manera provechosa. Y con favor que tuve de amigos y señores, todos mis trabajos y fatigas hasta entonces pasados fueron pagados con alcanzar lo que procuré: que fue un oficio real, viendo que no hay nadie que medre, sino los que le tienen (pp. 172–73).

The *asiento,* then, is an *oficio real,* a niche in the institutional hierarchy of civil government, which ascends to the king himself. Apparently aware even of the lowly nature of his new position, he is reluctant to name it and instead describes his duties one by one, declaring only at the final moment—with his clear and unambiguous *pregonero* voice—its identity: "pregonero, hablando en buen romance" (p. 173). The irony on the part of the author is unmistakable, as Bataillon and others have pointed out.[1] The intention is transparent. However, for Lázaro, who establishes the tone of his autobiography by setting himself up in opposition to those who "heredaron nobles estados," narrating his "trabajos y fatigas" through six *tratados,* beginning with nothing and ending up with an *oficio real* (no matter how demeaning it may seem to us or to his readers), his final royal office is perfectly appropriate and necessary in light of the use (abuse) to which he applies it.[2] It provides not only security and stability but also a camouflage for his activities as a hard-nosed, opportunistic businessman. He becomes a *mercader* who controls the buying and selling of one of Toledo's basic commodities.

In the sense that he operates behind his official role, acquiring money and favors from the labor of others, he is another *capellán:* ". . . en toda la ciudad, el que ha de echar vino a vender, o algo, si

---

[1]*Novedad,* p. 67 and n; Márquez Villanueva, "La actitud espiritual," p. 105 and n; Truman, "Lázaro de Tormes," p. 66: "Tiraqueau [*Commentarii de nobilitate, et iure primigeniorum,* Paris, 1549], on the authority of Cicero, Horace, and Juvenal, includes the office of *praeco* among those 'artes quibus nobilitati derogatur.' "

[2]As an *oficio real* it is also an honorable position. Cf. Márquez Villanueva, "La actitud espiritual," p. 97; García de la Concha, "La intención religiosa," p. 273: "No se puede perder la vista la creencia común de que cualquier oficio real bastaba para dar honra." The idea that Lázaro's "success" may be praised by none, yet is worthy of praise, seems to echo—ironically—Cicero's concern in *De Officiis* (ed. and trans. Walter Miller, Loeb Classical Library [London, 1913]): "Quibus ex rebus conflatur et efficitur id, quod quaerimus, honestum, quod etiamsi nobilitatum non sit, tamen honestum sit, quodque vere dicimus, etiamsi a nullo laudetur, natura esse laudabile" (p. 17). In other words, Lázaro seems to be emphasizing, not the nature of the position, but the fact that it was *he* who attained the position.

Lázaro de Tormes no entiende en ello, hacen cuenta de no sacar provecho." He is the source of the profit of others, and it is doubtful that he serves as their broker for nothing. He is able to be a *mercader* without being identified as such and thus escapes the voices "de los que dizen que [*ser mercader*] es peligroso al anima" and "que no es honroso."[3] The compatibility he detects between *pregonero* and *mercader* is based on the honor that a royal office brings and the profit gained by controlling a central part of Toledo's economy. He appropriates the governmentally sanctioned power of his voice to convert wine into profit just as in the third *tratado* he transformed his beggar's language into bread for himself and the *escudero*.

The perfect situation—the "cumbre de toda buena fortuna"—that Lázaro has created for himself, serving the king with one hand and himself with the other, is not perfect at all. He is not satisfied with the gains he has made, and it is the nature of this dissatisfaction, so clearly described by Bartolomé de Albornoz in another connection, that leads to the *caso* and to the origins of his *Vida*:

> en Hespaña . . . en uno se hallan siete y ocho oficios, que tan presto como es calçetero, quando comiença a entender aquel oficio y tracto que le hauia de luzir, tan presto le dexa, y le haze mercader, y en siendo mercader . . . hele que aspira para caballero. . . . [4]

In search of further "bien y favor" (p. 174), he agrees to take part in a business deal contrived by the archpriest. He is in effect bought by another *mercader,* who offers *honra* and *provecho* in exchange for Lázaro's service as a *criado.* This is not an informal arrangement, one that can be dissolved by consent of both parties; it is formally validated through a sacred contract that binds Lázaro to the archpriest's *criada* and thus to the archpriest permanently: " . . . procuró casarme con una criada suya. . . . Y así me casé con ella, y hasta agora no estoy

---

[3]Bartolomé de Albornoz, *Arte de los contratos* (Valencia, 1573), fol. 128. (I wish to acknowledge the direct contribution of Javier Herrero, who supplied me with a xerox copy of several folios of Albornoz's work.) See Herrero's recent article, "The Ending of *Lazarillo*: The *Wine* against the *Water,*" *MLN* 93 (1978): 313–19. Cf. Américo Castro, *Hacia Cervantes,* pp. 92–93, which cites a relevant passage from Rodrigo Sánchez de Arévalo's *Espejo de la vida humana* (Zaragoza, 1491): " 'No sin causa o sin misterio este nombre, honra, se escribe con *h,* la cual no se puede pronunciar sino con muy grande aspiración de las entrañas; por lo cual claramente se muestra ser natural cosa a los hombres el deseo de la honra e el ir tras ella' (fol. llv.). Pero honrosa caballería se derrumba: 'Por cierto, el moderno estudio de los caballeros se es vuelto a todo lo contrario, ca estudian e velan en ver a quien dañarán . . . e no se contentan de deshonrar la arte de la caballería . . . fázense mercaderes, la cual arte en ellos es sucia, vil e diforme' (fol 23v)."

[4]*Arte de los contratos,* fol. 129.

arrepentido" (*ibid.*). The benefits that result from the marriage ("trigo," "carne," "bodigos," "calzas viejas," and "una casilla par de la suya") soon become worthless because of the "malas lenguas" of his neighbors, which prevent him from enjoying them. In the form of gossip then, language, inserts itself into his comfortable life, disrupting his marriage and threatening the source of his material good fortune.

His protection from the rumors that attack his life is the underlying subject not only of this final *tratado* but of his entire *Vida*. His attempt to consolidate his "prosperidad" and "buena fortuna" is disclosed through his effort to silence the community around him. Or to put it another way, he will deafen himself by suppressing their voices so that he will not hear the damaging accusations made against his wife and thus himself. It is the archpriest, however, and not Lázaro, who suggests such a strategy. And as if to emphasize his master's responsibility, Lázaro reproduces their conversation so that Vuestra Merced may "hear" for himself:

> —Lázaro de Tormes, quien ha de mirar a dichos de malas lenguas nunca medrará. Digo esto porque no me maravillaría alguno, viendo entrar en mi casa a tu mujer y salir della. Ella entra muy a tu honra y suya, y esto te lo prometo. Por tanto, no mires a lo que puedan decir, sino a lo que te toca, digo, a tu provecho (p. 175).

It is only after the archpriest tells Lázaro not to *look at* what evil tongues are saying that the previous "no sé qué y sí sé que" of the rumors becomes clear:

> —Señor—le dije—, yo determiné de arrimarme a los buenos. Verdad es que algunos de mis amigos me han dicho algo deso, y aun por más de tres veces me han certificado que antes que comigo casase había parido tres veces, hablando con reverencia de Vuestra Merced, porque está ella delante (pp. 175–76).

Even a superficial reading of these two passages reveals different attitudes toward the rumors. While Lázaro dwells on their accuracy in regard to the archpriest's involvement ("Verdad es . . . tres veces me han certificado . . . "), the archpriest converts their truthful nature into potentially harmful effects on Lázaro's material benefits. In other words, as a priest he instructs his servant to perceive the rumors as words only. It is the archpriest's power over speech that turns *honra* into *provecho*, instantly negating that conventionally incompatible relationship between them: "Honra y provecho no caben en un saco." [5]

---

[5]Correas, *Vocabulario de refranes*, p. 170b.

To put it another way, *honra* and *provecho*, do not commingle; Lázaro's honor *is* his profit ("lo que te toca, digo, a tu provecho"). Honor becomes profit because the archpriest says it does.

The power of the archpriest's speech to transform words into things functions at another, far more crucial level. He subverts the relationship between speaking and hearing by referring to the gossip as a visible sign system, to be seen and not heard. Thus he blinds his servant when he tells him not to *look at* what others say ("quien ha de *mirar* a dichos de malas lenguas . . . no *mires* a lo que puedan *decir*") but to *feel* only those things that can *touch* him ("sino a lo que te *toca*"). By speaking the language of blindness, he is turning Lázaro into a blind man, limiting his access to any reality beyond what he tells him to believe and the *provecho* he offers. Such a literal reading of the archpriest's figural speech is not only admissible but required in the light of the fundamental roles that speaking and hearing have played from the beginning of Lázaro's *Vida*. The same conception of language as *verbum visibile* deceived Lázaro into consuming the accidents instead of the substance of the priest's bread in the second *tratado*. Moreover, it betrayed the *escudero* in the third and communicated Lázaro's status as an "hombre de bien" to the larger community in Toledo. This blindness is characteristic of the language of honor, which establishes one's worth in the *eyes* of others.

It is therefore vulnerable above all to those eyes that define honor, in this case to the gossipers whose voices disrupt the arrangement between Lázaro, the archpriest, and his *criada* and whose rumors the three conspire to suppress by their self-imposed silence:

(1) Lázaro: " . . . *veen* a mi mujer irle a hacer la cama y guisalle de comer" (p. 175).
(2) Archpriest: " . . . *viendo* entrar en mi casa a tu mujer y salir della" (*ibid.*, emphasis mine).
(3) Lázaro: " . . . yo holgaba y había por bien de que ella entrase y saliere, de noche y de día" (p. 176).

The absence of any reference in Lázaro's final remark to the prying eyes of his neighbors is traceable directly to a promise made by the archpriest, a promise that focuses our attention on the language of honor and its genetic relationship to the *caso*: "Ella entra muy a tu honra y suya, y esto te lo prometo . . . , digo, a tu provecho" (p. 175). If Lázaro controls the *provecho* of all those in the city who seek to sell their goods, his is in turn controlled by the archpriest. An explicit equivalent is drawn between his wife and his well-being. His wife must be

[90]

protected and her "honor" (public reputation) defended because she functions as a sign of his profit. The archpriest's equation is nearly mathematical in nature: *criada=honra=provecho.*

Lázaro is blinded by his master and silenced by his wife.[6] She threatens to destroy their mutually productive relationship after hearing the rumors enunciated in her presence. Her anger is placated only with Lázaro's promise of silence: " . . . cesó su llanto, con juramento que le hice de nunca más en mi vida mentalle nada de aquello . . . " (p. 176). The depth of his silence is emphasized with the use of the verb *mentar* rather than with *decir* or *hablar*: " . . . dezimos no mentéis tal cosa, que es no la nombréis ni os pase por la mente o el pensamiento." [7] It is not merely absolute silence that he promises but an eradication of the offending "aquello," that notorious sexual liaison between his wife and master. Here too, then, silence attempts to cover over sexual promiscuity, and it is because of his obsession with imposing silence on others that the *pregonero* of Toledo becomes a mute in his own home.

Just as the archpriest and his *criada* turn on Lázaro to maintain silence, so Lázaro himself turns on others to demand their participation in the conspiracy:

> Hasta el día de hoy nunca nadie nos oyó sobre el caso; antes, cuando alguno siento que quiere decir algo della [his wife], le atajo y le digo:
> —Mirá, si sois amigo, no me digáis cosa con que me pese, que no tengo por mi amigo al que me hace pesar (*ibid.*).

His technique should be familiar, for it is the same one he used against the *ciego*. His attempts to take away their voices in the way he removed the blind man's linguistic access to reality. This time, however, he has something more tangible with which to silence their gossip: friendship. He places the value of his friendship (and most likely their *provecho*) on their decision to speak or to be silent. And should this threat not close the mouths of his friends, he will back up his remarks with physical violence: "Quien otra cosa me dijere, yo me mataré con él. Desta manera no me dicen nada y yo tengo paz en mi casa" (pp. 176–77). The

---

[6]Gilman, "Death of Lazarillo," p. 156, states that Lázaro's final situation is "one of willful blindness. He refuses to see what is going on in his house, and he describes his surrender as an example of virtue." I do not intend to be overly casuistic, but it seems advisable to distinguish between what we perceive and what Vuestra Merced is supposed to perceive. Lázaro's blindness is made to appear to be a result of the archpriest's guidance. It is profitable for Lázaro to be blind, not only to please his master but also to protect his Christian marriage. The irony is obvious.

[7]Sebastián de Covarrubias, *Tesoro de la lengua castellana o española*, ed. Martín de Riquer (Barcelona, 1943), S.V. "mentar."

coward Lázaro finds himself in a much more "peligroso oficio" than the one he abandoned when he left the *alguacil*. Sticks and stones may break his bones, but words inflict even more serious damage.

The violence to which he says he is willing to resort underscores the power of the language of honor. He behaves as if he had the honor to defend, that is, as if he had the right and authority of that social class for which such a defense is reserved. He has appropriated the linguistic behavior of a "señor de título," for his remark "si sois amigo, no me digáis cosa con que me pese," is strangely reminiscent of the *escudero*'s reaction to Toledo's nobility:

> Ya cuando asienta un hombre con un señor de título, todavía pasa su laceria.... Por Dios, si con él topase, muy gran su privado pienso que fuese, y que mil servicios le hiciese, porque yo sabría mentille tan bien como otro, y agradalle a las mil maravillas; . . . *nunca decirle cosa con que le pesase, aunque mucho le cumpliese* . . . (p. 151, emphasis mine).

Moreover, his association of friendship, the defense of his dishonored wife, and the language he uses to claim redress echo the ancient legal rights reserved to *hidalgos* who were involved in cases of *desafío*:

> Deshonrra, o tuerto, o daño faziendo vn hidalgo a otro, puedelo desafiar por ello en esta manera, diziendo: Tornovos el amistad, e desafiovos, por tal deshonrra, o tuerto, o daño, que fezistes a mi, o a fulano mi pariente, porque he derecho de lo acaloñar.[8]

Even his use of the word *asiento* to refer to his *oficio real* is an obvious attempt to dignify an office unworthy of any honor. *Plazas de asiento*— "offices with life tenure that provided the office-holder with retirement at half-pay after twenty years of service" [9] were limited to *letrados* and defined substantial government positions such as those of *oidor, fiscal*, and *alcalde*, not local municipal *oficios* at the bottom of the hierarchy. Lázaro's honor is the language of honor he speaks, the clothes he wears, and the personal association he claims: "Esto fue el mesmo año que *nuestro* victorioso Emperador en esta insigne ciudad de Toledo entró, y tuvo en ella Cortes, y se hicieron grandes regocijos, como Vuestra Merced habrá oído" (p. 177). Lázaro constructs his *Vida* so that the final image with which Vuestra Merced leaves the text is one of celebration ("regocijos"), victory ("victorioso Emperador"), pros- peity ("prosperidad"), and exceptionally good fortune ("cumbre de toda buena fortuna"). It is clear, however, that at the time Lázaro

[8]*Las siete partidas*, in *Los códigos españoles concordados y anotados*, ed. Antonio de San Martín, 2d ed., 12 vols. (Madrid, 1872–73), 4:358.
[9]Richard Kagan, *Students and Society in Early Modern Spain* (Baltimore, 1974), p. 80.

writes his *Vida* his situation points to a much less optimistic interpretation.[10] In the careers of both Charles V and Lázaro de Tormes celebrations and good fortune seem to be things of the past: "Esto *fue* . . . en esta insigne ciudad de Toledo *entró*, y *tuvo* . . . y *se hicieron* grandes regocijos. . . . Pues *en este tiempo estaba*. . . . " This string of past tenses associated with good times contrasts strongly with the present tenses of Lázaro's speaking voice, through which he expresses his uneasy domestic peace: "Y así, me casé con ella y *hasta agora no estoy arrepentido*" (p. 174); "*Hasta el día de hoy* nunca nadie nos oyó sobre el caso" (p. 176); "Desta manera *no me dicen nada y yo tengo paz en mi casa*" (p. 177). He has been successful in stilling the voices of his tormentors until Vuestra Merced makes his request. He now faces a new challenge, a challenge unlike the others in that writing must bear the persuasive power of his voice. It must speak for itself, as it were, and in so doing by definition deprives Lázaro of a face-to-face encounter with Vuestra Merced. Simultaneously, however, such a request opens up another opportunity to deprive the gossipers of the power of their voices, namely, the opportunity to silence perhaps the most powerful voice of all, the only one that can touch Lázaro directly: the voice of Vuestra Merced. The very fact that he has asked Lázaro *in writing* to respond *in writing*, together with the fact that Lázaro obeys him, reveals a special relationship between them that exists outside as well as inside the report. Is Vuestra Merced conducting a *pesquisa* of the affair like the one executed by the *mayordomo* of the Comendador de la Magdalena? Does he have the authority to administer similar justice? And if so, will he base it on the document that Lázaro has prepared? Or, does he see himself as part of the *caso*? Is he, too, somehow a victim of the gossip, of the dishonor associated with Lázaro and the archpriest?

Asking such questions assumes, of course, that the narrative framework (the patron-servant device) is an integral part of the narrative itself, that is, that it plays a role as central to the interpretation—and hence to the meaning of the text—as the *tratados*. In other words, Vuestra Merced's presence is not merely to produce the text we have been reading, for on the contrary, it is the text that produces him. Similarly, it is inconceivable, to me at least, that he asks Lázaro to treat the *caso* "muy por extenso" out of idle curiosity. Lázaro does not take his request lightly; otherwise it is doubtful that he would have linked the "entera noticia" of his *persona* or his bold remark about those who inherit noble estates so firmly with the *caso*. Finally, the fact

[10]Woodward, "Author-Reader Relationship," p. 51.

that Vuestra Merced asks for a written report concerning the gossip he has already heard about *his* friend, the archpriest of San Salvador, indicates a special interest that can only be articulated through a further elaboration of the *caso* itself.[11] Lázaro's final reference to the way he handles his friend(s), together with the domestic peace it effects, may suggest an answer.

Lázaro begins the narration of the events that lead to the *caso* by explicitly establishing a structure of service relationships. The first is between himself and Vuestra Merced: "En el cual [oficio real] el día de hoy vivo y resido *a servicio* de Dios *y de Vuestra Merced*" (p. 173). This relationship echoes or is echoed by—depending on whether the *prólogo* is read as a prologue or epilogue—the manner in which Lázaro submits his *Vida* to Vuestra Merced: "Suplico a Vuestra Merced reciba *el pobre servicio de mano* de quien lo hiciera más rico si su poder y deseo se conformaran" (p. 89).[12] The second relationship is slightly more complex because Lázaro places the archpriest between himself and Vuestra Merced: "En este tiempo, viendo mi habilidad y buen vivir, teniendo noticia de mi persona el señor arcipreste de Sant Salvador, *mi señor, y servidor y amigo de Vuestra Merced* . . . (pp. 173–74). Lázaro serves Vuestra Merced; he also serves the archpriest, who serves Vuestra Merced, and there is a tightly bound service structure, a hierarchy with Vuestra Merced at the top and Lázaro at the bottom. This hierarchy is abolished almost instantly, however, with Lázaro's addition of the word *amigo*. While the archpriest is the "servidor" of Vuestra Merced, he is simultaneously his peer because of their friendship. Moreover, they are equals in Lázaro's eyes because he addresses them both as "vuestra merced." He focuses on their shared relationship—not on their master-servant status—in reminding Vuestra Merced of the binding power of friendship. His strategy is to make them the same by association (*amicorum esse communia omnia*), to force them to stand together in the midst of the scandal that has survived all effort at suppression.

While Lázaro associates his two masters, he is at the same time isolating himself from the source of the *caso*, the archpriest. A careful reading of the context in which reference is made to the *caso* reveals

[11]Rico, *Punto de vista*, p. 23n, states that "el *caso* que interesa a Vuestra Merced es, al fin, la clave de su propia relación con Lázaro." See Richard Hitchcock, "Lazarillo and 'Vuestra Merced,' " *MLN* 86 (1971): 264–66: "Vuestra Merced is interested in the behaviour of the archpriest, and not in Lázaro at all" (p. 265).

[12]Guillén, "La disposición," p. 268: "La redacción del *Lazarillo* es ante todo un acto de obediencia."

Lázaro's attempt to place the responsibility for the entire affair on the archpriest: "Hasta el día de hoy nunca nadie nos oyó sobre el caso; antes, cuando alguno siento que quiere decir algo della, le atajo . . . " (p. 176). The *caso* refers to the comings and goings of his wife, allegedly to "hacer [le al arcipreste] la cama y guisalle de comer" (p. 175). These activities did not begin after her marriage to Lázaro, however, for he explicitly states that his friends have informed him ("me han dicho") that she and the archpriest were sexually involved long before Lázaro arrived on the scene: " . . . que *antes* que comigo casase había parido tres veces" (p. 176). In other words, Lázaro is victimized, he implies, by an already existing scandal. He is like Vuestra Merced, who also hears the rumors about the archpriest's behavior *after* they have circulated throughout the parish. That the archpriest is ultimately culpable is further suggested by a series of remarks some of which we touched upon earlier:

(1) He and not Lázaro, suggested the marriage: ". . . procuró casarme con una criada suya" (p. 174).
(2) He made Lázaro and his wife rent a house next to his own: ". . . hizonos alquilar una casilla par de la suya" (p. 175).
(3) He tells Lázaro not to be concerned about the gossip: ". . .no mires a lo que puedan decir" (*ibid.*)
(4) He is cursed by Lázaro's wife for marrying them: "Y después tomôse a llorar y a echar maldiciones sobre quien comigo la habia casado" (p. 176).

The *caso* most narrowly defined by Lázaro is the sexual affair between the archpriest and his wife; he is involved by association, but even his association (marriage) was arranged by the archpriest. He does not traffic in sex; he merely profits from it. His defense of his wife, although cast in the language of a dishonored husband, is in reality based on the potential loss of his *provecho*. Thus his violent reaction toward his "friend" when he wants to talk about his wife is an attempt to protect his marriage, which, as we remarked previously, is the contractualized profit-sharing agreement between himself and the archpriest. His professed love for her ("es la *cosa* del mundo que yo más quiero" [*ibid.*]) is in reality his love of the benefits she produces. The "mil mercedes" he gains are the gifts presented to him by the archpriest. She is "tan buena mujer como vive dentro de las puertas de Toledo" (*ibid.*) because she has enabled him to associate with "los buenos," to become one of them. Finally his swearing to her "bondad," no matter how ironic to us or to Lázaro himself, restores domestic peace, the only environment in which the archpriest's "bien y favor" continue to supply Lázaro's "honra y provecho." Silence points to the economic foundation of honor and to the sexual promiscuity on which it is based.[13]

Honor, however, is ultimately the property of the community at large and is subject to continuous affirmation or attack. ("Quid est honestas nisi honor perpetuus ad aliquem secundo populi rumore delatus?" asks Lactantius.[14]) The rumors of Lázaro's neighbors, although true, are spoken by "*malas* lenguas," for they threaten the source of his "*buena* fortuna." More important, they bind together a new *ménage à trois*: the archpriest, Lázaro, and Vuestra Merced. Lázaro's *honra / provecho* survives only if Vuestra Merced perceives the archpriest's dishonor as defining his own. When Lázaro speaks to his friend ("—Mirá, si sois amigo, no me digáis cosa con que me pese, que no tengo por mi amigo al que me hace pesar") he is simultaneously speaking to his master's friend. He is telling Vuestra Merced what the archpriest told him, echoing the strategy he used in the third *tratado* when he communicated the *escudero*'s fiction to the *escribano* in order to remove himself from a perilous situation.

Such an interpretation of Vuestra Merced's role in *Lázaro*'s life may be based on an overemphasis on the meaning of the word *amigo*. But how else are we to explain the motivations of Vuestra Merced's request that Lázaro remain silent about the *caso* by writing his report?[15] Vuestra Merced reads it in privacy and silence and thereby precludes the possibility of being seen together with Lázaro (wearing the archpriest's stockings no doubt) in the necessary physical confrontation of an oral report. The letter binds as well as separates. It forces Vuestra Merced to become part of the *caso* yet enables him to stand literally apart from it. In the act of writing to his friend's servant he initiates his participation in the knowledge of the dishonored status of his friend. And in the act of reading Lázaro's response, he possesses and is possessed by its dishonoring truth. Vuestra Merced is part of the *Lazarillo*'s narrative complicity and therefore of its author's language and life. If the *prólogo* functions as the final *tratado*, then Lázaro's "buen puerto" bespeaks the safety he envisions in fulfilling Vuestra Merced's

[13]García de la Concha is absolutely correct when he describes the association of honor, profit, and "los buenos" with the "nueva mentalidad de la sociedad dineraria" ("La intención religiosa," p. 273).

[14]*Divinarum Institutionum* 3. 8. 39. For honor and "opinión" in Spain, see Américo Castro, *De la edad conflictiva* (Madrid, 1961), pp. 79–99.

[15]I am of course talking about the illusion of the book; obviously there would be no *Vida* had Lázaro told Vuestra Merced his story orally.

request. That is, if his "buen puerto" is read as a narrative act, it points to the success of his linguistic enterprise: His salvation is brought about through himself as *écriture*. Lázaro's *Vida* may well be more than just an analogy to the pardoner's *bulas*: His narrative is a sign that points to his salvation and to his signified life as writer.

It has been argued that the *Lazarillo de Tormes* is a comic book.[16] Underneath its comedy, its "tono cordial y regocijado," [17] as we have attempted to demonstrate, exists a serious interest in language and its power to articulate both literal and metaphorical worlds. The absence of Lázaro's final "father," the anonymous author, is the result of a conscious rejection of the book's paternity.[18] Unlike his narrator, the author was not obsessed with the public honor and glory produced by his narrative.[19] He was obviously content to enjoy in secret the praise of his immediate audience as they read the book, and perhaps even more significant, he was safe in the knowledge of his invulnerability to the potentially destructive power of its language. While this self-imposed anonymity seems to have neutralized the institutional power of inquisitorial censorship, the *Lazarillo* was not as fortunate. In 1559 it was censored altogether and reduced to an entry in the *Catalogus librorum qui prohibentur*. Not until 1573 was it released as a somewhat less potent book. The author may well have been the *Lazarillo*'s best, most careful reader, for he seemed to have been aware that its language constituted more than humorous fiction. He clearly saw the implications in saying / writing, *Hoc est meum liber.*

[16]This is the opinion of most readers. Rico, however, sounds a note of caution: " . . . tampoco me satisface enteramente la interpretación de nuestra novela como simple *obra de burlas*" (*La novela picaresca española*, pp. lxiii–lxiv).

[17]Lázaro Carreter, *Lazarillo*, p. 192.

[18]This was a metaphor of the time; Castro, *Hacia Cervantes*, p. 102: "El escritor [del siglo XVI] conoce su esfuerzo y lo pregona. Díaz Tanco habla así de sus libros: 'compuestos, trazados, asentados, limados, fulminados y perfeccionados con mi punto y tijera, e ansí les llamo los míos amados hijos legítimos, engendrados en mi vejez, con los cuales olvido las pasiones mundanas.' "

[19]Gilman, "Death of *Lazarillo*," p. 150.

# Bibliography

The following bibliography lists only those studies cited and/or consulted. For a more complete bibliography on the *Lazarillo de Tormes*, see A. D. Deyermond, *"Lazarillo de Tormes": A Critical Guide* (London, 1975); see also Joseph Laurenti, *Bibliografía de la literatura picaresca* (Metuchen, N.J., 1973).

## I. Primary Sources. Editions and translations of the *Lazarillo de Tormes*.

Alpert, Michael. *Two Spanish Picaresque Novels: "Lazarillo," "The Swindler."* Harmondsworth, 1969.

Blecua, Alberto, ed. *La vida de Lazarillo de Tormes y de sus fortunas y adversidades.* Madrid, 1974.

Caso González, José, ed. *La vida de Lazarillo de Tormes y de sus fortunas y adversidades. Edición crítica.* Madrid, 1967. Anejos del Boletín de la Real Academia Española, vol. 17.

Cejador y Frauca, Julio, ed. *La vida de Lazarillo de Tormes y de sus fortunas y adversidades.* Madrid, 1914.

Guillén, Claudio, ed. *La vida de Lazarillo de Tormes y de sus fortunas y adversidades.* In *Lazarillo de Tormes and El Abencerraje*, pp. 53–106. New York, 1966.

Isasi Angulo, Amando, ed. *Lazarillo de Tormes.* Barcelona, 1970.

Jones, R. O., ed. *La vida de Lazarillo de Tormes y de sus fortunas y adversidades.* Manchester, 1963.

Ricapito, Joseph, ed. *La vida de Lazarillo de Tormes y de sus fortunas y adversidades.* Madrid, 1976.

Rico, Francisco, ed. *La vida de Lazarillo de Tormes y de sus fortunas y adversidades.* In *La novela picaresca española*, pp. 3–80. Barcelona, 1967.

————. *Lazarillo de Tormes.* Barcelona, 1976.

Rudder, Robert S. *The Life of Lazarillo de Tormes: His Fortunes and Misfortunes as Told by Himself with a Sequel by Juan de Luna.* New York, 1973.

## II. Secondary Sources.

Abrams, Fred. "A Note on the Mercedarian Friar in the *Lazarillo de Tormes.*" *Romance Notes* 11 (1969): 444–46.

Albornoz, Bartolomé de. *Arte de los contratos.* Valencia, 1573.

Alemán, Mateo. *Ortografía castellana.* Edited by J. R. Garcidueñas. Mexico City, 1950.

Ambrose, Saint. *Expositio Evangelii secundam Lucam.* Edited and translated by Dom Gabriel Tissot, O.S.B. Sources chrétiennes, vols. 45 (1956) and 52 (1958). Paris.

Apel, Karl. *Die Idee der Sprache in der Tradition des Humanismus von Dante bis Vico.* Bonn, 1963. Translated by Luciano Tosti as *L'idea di lingua nella tradizione dell'umanesimo da Dante a Vico.* Bologna, 1975.

Auerbach, Erich. "Figura." In *Scenes from the Drama of European Literature,* pp. 11–76. New York, 1959.

———. *Literary Language and Its Public in Late Latin Antiquity and in the Middle Ages.* Translated by Ralph Manheim. New York, 1965.

———. *Mimesis: The Representation of Reality in Western Literature.* Translated by Willard R. Trask. 1953. Reprint. New York, 1957.

Augustine, Saint. *De Trinitate.* In *Patrologiae cursus completus: Series latina,* edited by J. P. Migne. 221 vols. Paris, 1844–90. Vol. 42, col. 819–1098, 1886.

———. *Tractatus in Joannem.* In *Patrologiae cursus completus: Series latina,* edited by J. P. Migne, Paris, 1844–90. Vol. 35, col. 1379–1976, 1845.

Barthes, Roland. *Système de la mode.* Paris, 1967.

Bataillon, Marcel. *Novedad y fecundidad del "Lazarillo de Tormes."* Translated by Luis Cortés Vázquez. Salamanca, 1968.

Bennassar, Bartolomé. *Valladolid au siècle d'or: Une ville de Castille et sa campagne au XVIe siècle.* Paris and The Hague, 1967.

Benveniste, Emile. "L'Appareil formel de l'énonciation." *Langages* 17 (1970): 12–18.

———. "Nature du signe linguistique." In *Problèmes de linguistique générale,* pp. 49–55. Paris, 1966.

———. "Sémiologie de la langue." *Semiotica* 1 (1969): 1–12, 127–135.

Bernis Madrazo, Carmen. *Indumentaria española en tiempos de Carlos V.* Madrid, 1962.

Boccaccio. *De casibus virorum illustrum.* In *Opere in versi, Corbaccio, Trattatello in laude di Dante, Prose latine, Epistole,* edited by Pier Giorgio Ricci, pp. 785–891. Milan and Naples, 1965.

Bogatyrev, Petr. "Costume as Sign." In *Semiotics of Art: Prague School Contributions,* edited by Ladislav Matejka and Irwin R. Titunik, pp. 13–19. Cambridge, Mass., 1976.

Brandt, Aage. "Dom Juan ou la force de la parole: Essai sur le contrat." *Poétique* 12 (1973): 584–95.

Brown, R., and Gilman, A. "The Pronouns of Power and Stability." In *Language and Social Context: Selected Readings,* edited by Pier Paolo Giglioli, pp. 252–82. Harmondsworth, 1975.

Camporeale, Salvatore. *Lorenzo Valla: Umanesimo e teologia.* Florence, 1972.

Capella Martínez, Miguel. *La industria en Madrid: Ensayo histórico crítico de la fabricación y artesanía madrileñas.* 2 vols. Madrid, 1962.

Carey, Douglas M. "Asides and Interiority in *Lazarillo de Tormes.*" *Studies in Philology* 66 (1969): 119–34.

Carilla, Emilio. "Cuatro notas sobre el *Lazarillo*." *Revista de Filología Española* 43 (1960): 97–116.

Caro Baroja, Julio. "Honor y vergüenza (examen histórico de varios conflictos populares)." In *La ciudad y el campo*, pp. 63–130. Madrid, 1966.

Carrillo y Gariel, Abelardo. *El traje en la nueva España*. Mexico City, 1959.

Castan, Yves. *Honnêté et relations sociales en Languedoc (1715–1780)*. Paris, 1974.

Castro, Américo, "Algunas observaciones acerca del concepto del honor en los siglos XVI y XVII." *Revista de Filología Española* 3 (1916): 1–50, 357–86.

―――. *De la edad conflectiva*. Madrid, 1961.

―――. "El 'Lazarillo de Tormes.'" In *Hacia Cervantes*, pp. 143–66. 3d ed. Madrid, 1967.

Cavallera, Ferdinand. "L'interprétation du chapitre VI de Saint Jean: Une controverse exégétique au Concile de Trente." *Revue d'Histoire Ecclésiastique* 10 (1909): 687–709.

Cervantes, Miguel de. *La gitanilla*. In *Novelas ejemplares*, edited by Francisco Rodríguez Marín. 2 vols. 1914. Reprint. Madrid, 1962. Vol. 1, pp. 3–130.

Cicero. *De Inventione*. In *De Optimo genere oratorum, Topica*, edited and translated by H. M. Hubbell, pp. 1–346. Loeb Classical Library. London, 1949.

―――. *De Officiis*. Edited and translated by Walter Miller. Loeb Classical Library. London, 1913.

―――. *Pro Sestio*. In *Cicero: The Speeches: Pro Sestio and In Vatinium*, edited and translated by R. Gardner. Loeb Classical Library. London, 1958.

Corominas, Joan. *Diccionario crítico etimológico de la lengua castellana*. 4 vols. Bern, 1954.

Correas, Gonzalo. *Vocabulario de refranes y frases proverbiales*. Edited by Louis Combet. Bordeaux, 1967.

Covarrubias, Sebastián de. *Tesoro de la lengua castellana o española*. Edited by Martín de Riquer. Barcelona, 1943.

Culler, Jonathan. *Structuralist Poetics: Structuralism, Linguistics, and the Study of Literature*. Ithaca, 1975.

Curtius, Ernst Robert. *European Literature and the Latin Middle Ages*. Translated by Willard R. Trask. New York, 1953.

Derrida, Jacques. *De la grammatologie*. Paris, 1967.

Descartes, René. *De la dioptrique*. In *Oeuvres*, edited by C. Adam and P. Tannery. 11 vols. Paris, 1964–65. Vol. 6, pp. 79–228.

Deyermond, A. D. *"Lazarillo de Tormes": A Critical Guide*. London, 1975.

Ducrot, Oswald. *Dire et ne pas dire: Principes de sémantique linguistique*. Paris, 1972.

Dumoutet, Edouard. *Corpus Domini: Aux sources de la piété eucharistique médiévale*. Paris, 1942.

―――. *Le désir de voir l'hostie et les origines de la dévotion au Saint Sacrament*. Paris, 1926.

Dunn, Peter N. "Honour and the Christian Background in Calderón." In *Critical Essays on the Theatre of Calderón*, edited by Bruce W. Wardropper, pp. 24–60. New York, 1965.

———. "Pleberio's World." *PMLA* 91 (1976): 406–17.

Durand, Frank. "The Author and Lázaro: Levels of Comic Meaning." *Bulletin of Hispanic Studies* 45 (1968): 89–101.

Erasmus. *Lingua*. Translated by Bernardo Pérez de Chinchón. In *La lengua de Erasmo nuevamente romançada por muy elegante estilo*, edited by Dorothy S. Severin. Madrid, 1975.

Escobar, Juan de. *Romancero del Cid*. Edited by Carolina Michaelis Vasconcellos. Leipzig, 1875.

Fernández de Oviedo, Gonzalo. *Las quinquagenas de la nobleza de España*. Edited by Vicente de la Fuente. Madrid, 1880.

Fish, Stanley E. "How to Do Things with Austin and Searle: Speech Act Theory and Literary Criticism." *MLN* 91 (1976): 983–1025.

Freud, Sigmund. "Fetishism." In *The Standard Edition of the Complete Psychological Works of Sigmund Freud*, edited and translated by James Strachey (with Anna Freud). 24 vols. London, 1953–74. Vol. 21, pp. 152–57.

———. "My Views on the Part Played by Sexuality in the Aetiology of the Neuroses." In *The Standard Edition of the Complete Psychological Works of Sigmund Freud*, edited and translated by James Strachey (with Anna Freud). 24 vols. London, 1953–74. Vol. 7, pp. 271–79.

———. *The Interpretation of Dreams*. In *The Standard Edition of the Complete Psychological Works of Sigmund Freud*, edited and translated by James Strachey (with Anna Freud). 24 vols. London, 1953–74. Vols. 4 (pt. 1) and 5 (pt. 2).

Gans, Eric. *Essais d'esthétique paradoxale*. Paris, 1977.

García de la Concha, Víctor. "La intención religiosa del *Lazarillo*." *Revista de Filología Española* 55 (1972): 243–77.

García Valdecasas, Alfonso. *El hidalgo y el honor*. Madrid, 1948.

Gatti, José. *Introducción al "Lazarillo de Tormes."* Buenos Aires, 1968.

Gennep, Arnold von. *Manuel de folklore français contemporain*. 4 vols. Paris, 1937.

Gili Gaya, Samuel, ed. *Tesoro lexicográfico (1492–1726)*. Madrid, 1947.

Gillet, Joseph E. "A Note on the *Lazarillo de Tormes*." *MLN* 55 (1940): 130–34.

Gilman, Stephen. "The Death of *Lazarillo de Tormes*." *PMLA* 81 (1966): 149–66.

Goñi Gaztambide, José. *Historia de la Bula de la Cruzada en España*. Vitoria, 1958.

———. "Los cuestores en España y la regalía de indulgencias." *Hispania Sacra* 2 (1949): 3–45, 285–310.

Gray, Hanna E. "Renaissance Humanism: The Pursuit of Eloquence." In *Renaissance Essays from the Journal of the History of Ideas*, edited by Paul O. Kristeller and Philip P. Wiener, pp. 199–216. New York, 1968.

Guevara, Antonio de. *Aviso de privados o despertador de cortesanos*. Edited by A. Alvarez de la Villa. Paris, n.d.

Guillén, Claudio. "La disposición temporal del *Lazarillo de Tormes*." *Hispanic

*Review* 25 (1957): 264–79.

——. *Literature As System: Essays toward the Theory of Literary History.* Princeton 1971.

——. "Luis Sánchez, Ginés de Pasamonte y los inventores del género picaresco." In *Homenaje al Profesor Rodríguez-Moñino.* 2 vols. Madrid, 1966. Vol. 1, pp. 221–31.

Haedo, Diego de. *Topographia e historia general de Argel, repartida en cinco tratados.* Valladolid, 1612.

Hermosilla, Diego de. *Diálogo de la vida de los pajes de palacio.* Edited by Donald Mackenzie. Valladolid, 1916.

Herrero, Javier. "The Ending of *Lazarillo*: The *Wine* against the *Water.*" *MLN* 93 (1978): 313–19.

——. "The Great Icons of the *Lazarillo*: The Bull, the Wine, the Sausage and the Turnip." *Ideologies and Literature* 1, no. 5 (1978): 3–18.

Hitchcock, Richard. "Lazarillo and 'Vuestra Merced.'" *MLN* 86 (1971): 264–66.

Hoffman-Krayer, E., and Bächtold-Staubli, Hanns, eds. *Handwörterbuch des deutschen Aberglaubens.* 10 vols. Berlin and Leipzig, 1927–42.

Kagan, Richard. *Students and Society in Early Modern Spain.* Baltimore, 1974.

Lactantius. *Opera omnia.* Edited by Samuel Brandt. Prague, 1890.

Lapide, Cornelius à. *Commentaria in Lucam.* Antwerp, 1681.

Laplanche, J., and Pontalis, J.-B. *Vocabulaire de la psychanalyse.* Paris, 1967. Translated selections by Peter Kussell and Jeffrey Mehlman. In *French Freud: Structural Studies in Psychoanalysis*, pp. 179–202. Yale French Studies. New Haven, 1972.

Lausberg, Heinrich. *Manual de retórica literaria: Fundamentos de una ciencia de la literatura.* Translated by José Pérez Riesco. 3 vols. Madrid, 1966–68.

Lázaro Carreter, Fernando. *"Lazarillo de Tormes" en la picaresca.* Barcelona, 1972.

Lea, Henry Charles. *A History of Auricular Confessions and Indulgences in the Latin Church.* 3 vols. Philadelphia, 1896.

——. "Indulgences in Spain." *Papers of the American Society of Church History* 1 (1889): 129–71.

Leguina, Enrique de. *La espada: Apuntes para su historia en España.* Seville, 1885.

León, Luis de. *De los nombres de Cristo.* Edited by Federico de Onís. 3 vols. Madrid, 1914–34.

Leroi-Gourhan, André. *Le geste et la parole, I: Technique et langage.* Paris, 1964.

Lévi-Strauss, Claude. *Anthropologie structurale.* 2 vols. Paris, 1973.

Lida de Malkiel, María Rosa. "Función del cuento popular en el *Lazarillo de Tormes.*" In *Actas del primer congreso internacional de hispanistas*, edited by Cyril A. Jones and Frank Pierce, pp. 349–59. Oxford, 1964.

McGrady, Donald. "Social Irony in *Lazarillo de Tormes* and Its Implications for Authorship." *Romance Philology* 23 (1969–70): 557–67.

Mancing, Howard. "The Deceptiveness of *Lazarillo de Tormes.*" *PMLA* 90 (1975):

426–32.

Marasso, Arturo. "Aspectos del *Lazarillo de Tormes*." In *Estudios de literatura española*, pp. 175–86. Buenos Aires, 1955.

———. "La elaboración del *Lazarillo de Tormes*." In *Estudios de literatura española*, pp. 157–74. Buenos Aires, 1955.

Marin, Louis. *La critique du discours: Sur la "Logique de Port-Royal" et les "Pensées" de Pascal*. Paris, 1975.

Marín Ocete, Antonio. *El arzobispo don Pedro Guerrero y la política conciliar española en el siglo XVI*. 2 vols. Madrid, 1970.

Márquez Villanueva, Francisco. "La actitud espiritual del *Lazarillo de Tormes*." In *Espiritualidad y literatura en el siglo XVI*, pp. 69–137. Madrid, 1968.

Martz, Linda, and Porres Martín-Cleto, Julio. *Toledo y los toledanos en 1561*. Toledo, 1974.

Mehlman, Jeffrey. "How to Read Freud on Jokes: The Critic as *Schadchen*." *New Literary History* 6 (1974–75): 439–61.

Merleau-Ponty, Maurice. *Signs*. Translated by Richard McCleary. Evanston, 1964.

Minguet, Charles. *Recherches sur les structures narratives dans le "Lazarillo de Tormes*." Paris, 1970.

Molho, Maurice, ed. *Romans picaresques espagnols*. Paris, 1968. The introduction has been translated by Augusto Gálvez-Cañero y Pidal as *Introducción al pensamiento picaresco*. Salamanca, 1972.

Morreale, Margarita. "Reflejos de la vida española en el *Lazarillo*." *Clavileño* 30 (1954): 28–31.

Morris, C.B. "Lázaro and the Squire: 'Hombres de bien.'" *Bulletin of Hispanic Studies* 41 (1964): 238–41.

Mounin, Georges. *Introduction à la sémiologie*. Paris, 1970.

Nacht, Jacob. "The Symbolism of the Shoe with Special Reference to Jewish Sources." *The Jewish Quarterly Review* 6 (1915–16): 1–22.

*Novísima recopilación de las leyes de España*. 6 vols. Madrid, 1805–7.

Orozco, Alonso de. *De nueve nombres de Cristo*. In Luis de León, *De los nombres de Cristo*, edited by Federico de Onís. 3 vols. Madrid, 1914–34. Vol. 3, pp. 249–60.

Parker, A. A. "The Psychology of the *pícaro* in 'El *Buscón*.'" *Modern Language Review* 42 (1947): 58–69.

Perry, T. Anthony. "Biblical Symbolism in the *Lazarillo de Tormes*." *Studies in Philology* 67 (1970): 139–46.

Piper, Anson. "The 'Breadly Paradise' of *Lazarillo de Tormes*." *Hispania* 44 (1961): 269–71.

Pitt-Rivers, Julian. "Honour and Social Status." In *Honour and Shame: The Values of Mediterranean Society*, edited by J. G. Peristiany, pp. 19–77. Chicago, 1966.

Pla Cárceles, José. "La evolución del tratamiento 'Vuestra Merced.'" *Revista de Filología Española* 10 (1923): 245–80.

Prieto, Antonio. "De un símbolo, un signo y un síntoma (Lázaro, Guzmán, Pablos)." In *Ensayo semiológico de sistemas literarios*, pp. 15–65. Barcelona, 1972.

Puccini, Dario. "La struttura del *Lazarillo de Tormes*." *Annali della Facoltà di Lettere e Filosofia e Magistero dell'Università di Cagliari* 23 (1970): 65–103.

Quintilian. *Institutio oratoria*. Edited and translated by H.E. Butler. Loeb Classical Library. 4 vols. London, 1920–22.

Raitt, Jill. *The Eucharistic Theology of Theodore Beza*. Chambersburg, Pa., 1972.

Rasperger, Christopher, *Duccentae verborum: "Hoc est corpus meum" interpretatones*. Ingolstadt, 1577.

Redondo, Augustin. *Antonio de Guevara (1480?–1545) et L'Espagne de son temps*. Geneva, 1976.

Ricapito, Joseph V. "'Cara de Dios': Ensayo de rectificación." *Bulletin of Hispanic Studies* 50 (1973): 142–46.

———. "*Lazarillo de Tormes* (Chapter V) and Masuccio's Fourth *Novella*." *Romance Philology* 23 (1970): 305–11.

Rico, Francisco. *La novela picaresca y el punto de vista*. Barcelona, 1970.

———. "Problemas del 'Lazarillo.'" *Boletín de la Real Academia Española* 46 (1966): 277–96.

Rodríguez Marín, Francisco, ed. *12.600 refranes más no contenidos en la colección del maestro Gonzalo Correas*. Madrid, 1930.

Rodríguez Villa, Antonio. "Inventario del moviliario [*sic*] alhajas, ropas, armería y otros efectos del Señor Don Beltrán de la Cueva, tercer duque de Alburquerque. A. [ño] 1560." *Revista de Archivos, Bibliotecas y Museos* 9 (1883): 17–37, 66–80, 99–104.

Romani, Aquilae. *De figuris sententiarum et elocutionis liber*. In *Rhetores Latini minores*, edited by Karl Halm, pp. 22–37. Leipzig, 1863.

Ruegg, Walter. *Cicero und der Humanismus: Formale untersuchungen über Petrarca und Erasmus*. Zurich, 1946.

Ruffinatto, Aldo. *Struttura e significazione del "Lazarillo de Tormes": I; La costruzione del modello operativo. Dall'intreccio alla fabula*. Turin, 1975.

Rumeau, Aristide. *Le "Lazarillo de Tormes": Essai d'interprétation, essai d'attribution*. Paris, 1964.

———. "Notes au *Lazarillo:* 'Despedir la bula.'" *LNL* 163 (1962): 2–7.

Saez Piñuela, María José. *La moda en la corte de Felipe II*. Madrid, 1962.

San Martín, Antonio de, ed. *Los códigos españoles concordados y anotados*. 2d ed. 12 vols. Madrid, 1872–73. Vol. 4.

Sébillot, Paul. *Le folk-lore français*. 4 vols. Paris, 1904.

Seigel, Jerrold E. *Rhetoric and Philosophy in Renaissance Humanism: The Union of Eloquence and Wisdom, Petrarch to Valla*. Princeton, 1968.

Sicroff, Albert. "Sobre el estilo del *Lazarillo de Tormes*." *Nueva Revista de Filología Hispánica* 11 (1957): 157–70.

Sieber, Harry. *The Picaresque*. London, 1977.

Simone, Raffaele. "Sémiologie augustinienne." *Semiotica* 6 (1972): 1−31.

Sobejano, Gonzalo. "Un perfil de las picaresca: El pícaro hablador." In *Studia Hispanica in Honorem R. Lapesa.* 3 vols. Madrid, 1972. Vol. 3, pp. 467−85.

Stekel, Wilhelm. *Sexual Aberrations: The Phenomena of Fetishism in Relation to Sex.* Translated by S. Parker. 2 vols. New York, 1952.

Straparola, Giovan Francesco. *Le piacevoli notti.* Edited by Giuseppe Rua. 2 vols. Bari, 1927.

Terlingen, Juan. "Cara de Dios." In *Studia Philologica: Homenaje ofrecido a Dámaso Alonso.* 3 vols. Madrid, 1963. Vol. 3, pp. 463−78.

Todorov, Tzvetan. "On Linguistic Symbolism." Translated by Richard Klein. *New Literary History* 6 (1974): 111−34.

Torquemada, Antonio de. *Coloquios satíricos.* Edited by M. Menéndez Pelayo. Nueva Biblioteca de Autores Españoles, vol. 7, pp. 485−581. Madrid, 1907.

―――. *Manual de escribientes.* Edited by María Josefa C. de Zamora and A. Zamora Vicente. Madrid, 1970.

Truman, R. W. "*Lazarillo de Tormes,* Petrarch's *De remediis fortunae,* and Erasmus's *Praise of Folly.*" *Bulletin of Hispanic Studies* 52 (1975): 33−53.

―――. "Lázaro de Tormes and the *Homo Novus* Tradition." *Modern Language Review* 64 (1969): 62−67.

―――. "Parody and Irony in the Self-Portrayal of Lázaro de Tormes." *Modern Language Review* 63 (1968): 600−605.

Velasco Bayon, Balbino. *Historia de Cuéllar.* Segovia, 1974.

Volosinov, V. N. *Marxism and the Philosophy of Language.* Translated by Ladislav Matejka and Irwin R. Titunik. New York, 1973.

Wardropper, Bruce W. "El trastorno de la moral en el *Lazarillo.*" *Nueva Revista de Filología Hispánica* 15 (1961): 441−47.

―――. "The Strange Case of Lázaro Gonzáles Pérez." *MLN* 92 (1977): 202−12.

Waterworth, J., trans. *The Canons and Decrees of the Sacred Oecumenical Council of Trent. . . .* London, 1848.

Weisser, Michael. "Les marchands de Tolède dans l'économie castillane, 1565−1635." *Mélanges de la Casa de Velázquez* 7 (1971): 223−32.

―――. "The Decline of Castile Revisited: The Case of Toledo." *The Journal of European Economic History* 2 (1973): 614−40.

―――. *The Peasants of the Montes: The Roots of Rural Rebellion in Spain.* Chicago, 1976.

Willis, Raymond S. "Lazarillo and the Pardoner: The Artistic Necessity of the Fifth *Tractado.*" *Hispanic Review* 27 (1959): 267−79.

Woodward, L.J. "Author-Reader Relationship in the *Lazarillo de Tormes.*" *Forum for Modern Language Studies* 1 (1965): 43−53.

[105]

# Index

Marin, Louis, x, 53 n
Márquez Villanueva, Francisco, 32 n, 60 n
Martín-Cleto, Julio Porres, 32 n
Martz, Linda, 32 n
Merleau-Ponty, Maurice, 61 n
Minguet, Charles, 10 n
Molho, Maurice, xiv n, 10 n, 20 n, 36 n, 78 n
Morris, C. B., 80 n
Mounin, Georges, xi n

Orozco, Alonso de, 22 n

Paradox, 11–14 *passim*, 30, 45, 59
Parker, A. A., 3 n
Pérez de Chinchón, Bernardo, viii n, 1 n
Pérez de Lara, Alonso, 66
Petrarch, F., ix n
Pitt-Rivers, Julian, ix
Pontalis, J. -B., 3 n, 5 n

Quintilian, x n, 31, 60 n, 68

Raitt, Jill, 24 n, 25 n, 26
Ricapito, Joseph V., 22 n
Rico, Francisco, vii n, xii n, xiv n, 9 n, 13 n, 31 n, 46 n, 53 n, 63 n, 64 n, 82 n, 94 n
Rodríguez Marín, Francisco, 74 n
Romani, Aquilae, 45

Sébillot, Paul, 52
Sicroff, Albert, 78 n
Siegmar, Gotthilf Carl (Dr. Aigremont), 51
Simone, Raffaele, 25 n
Sobejano, Gonzalo, ix n
Stekel, Wilhelm, 51 n, 52
Straparola, Giovan Francesco, 52

Todorov, Tzvetan, 25 n
Torquemada, Antonio de, ix n, xii n, xiii n, 81, 82
Truman, R. W., vii n, 23 n, 80 n, 87 n

Urrea, Jerónimo de, 42

Volosinov, V. N., 39 n

Wardropper, Bruce W., 3 n, 4 n
Weisser, Michael, 32 n
Woodward, L. J., 6 n, 15 n

THE JOHNS HOPKINS UNIVERSITY PRESS


This book was composed in Linocomp II Baskerville by Coda Press, Inc., from a design by Charles West. It was printed on 55 lb. Publishers Offset Cream and bound by The Maple Press Company.

**Library of Congress Cataloging in Publication Data**

Sieber, Harry.
  Language and society in La vida de Lazarillo de Tormes.

  Bibliography: pp. 98−105
  Includes index.
  1. Lazarillo de Tormes.   I.  Title.
PQ6409.S53      863′.3          78−8425
ISBN 0−8018−2121−5